THE LUCENT LIBRARY OF SCIENCE AND TECHNOLOGY

The Internet

by Peggy J. Parks

LUCENT BOOKS
An imprint of Thomson Gale, a part of The Thomson Corporation

THOMSON
— ★ —
GALE

Detroit • New York • San Francisco • San Diego • New Haven, Conn. • Waterville, Maine • London • Munich

LIBRARY OF CONGRESS CATALOGING-IN-PUBLICATION DATA

Parks, Peggy J., 1951–
  The Internet / by Peggy J. Parks.
    p. cm. — (Lucent library of science & technology)
  Includes bibliographical references and index.
  ISBN 1-59018-441-6 (alk. paper)
  1. Internet—Juvenile literature. I. Title. II. Series: Lucent library of science and technology.
  TK5105.875.I57P3825 2005
  004.67'8—dc22
                                                                  2005000075

Printed in the United States of America

Table of Contents

Foreword   4

Introduction   7
The World on a Desktop

Chapter 1   12
The Roots of the Internet

Chapter 2   26
Enter the World Wide Web

Chapter 3   39
How the Internet Works

Chapter 4   53
A Million and One Uses

Chapter 5   68
The Dark Side

Chapter 6   82
A Changing World

Notes   96

Glossary   100

For Further Reading   102

Works Consulted   104

Index   107

Picture Credits   112

About the Author   112

Foreword

"The world has changed far more in the past 100 years than in any other century in history. The reason is not political or economic, but technological—technologies that flowed directly from advances in basic science."

— Stephen Hawking, "A Brief History of Relativity," *Time,* 2000

The twentieth-century scientific and technological revolution that British physicist Stephen Hawking describes in the above quote has transformed virtually every aspect of human life at an unprecedented pace. Inventions unimaginable a century ago have not only become commonplace but are now considered necessities of daily life. As science historian James Burke writes, "We live surrounded by objects and systems that we take for granted, but which profoundly affect the way we behave, think, work, play, and in general conduct our lives."

For example, in just one hundred years, transportation systems have dramatically changed. In 1900 the first gasoline-powered motorcar had just been introduced, and only 144 miles (232km) of U.S. roads were hard-surfaced. Horse-drawn trolleys still filled the streets of American cities. The airplane had yet to be invented. Today 217 million vehicles speed along 4 million miles (6.4 million km) of U.S. roads. Humans have flown to the moon and commercial aircraft are capable of transporting passengers across the Atlantic Ocean in less than three hours.

The transformation of communications has been just as dramatic. In 1900 most Americans lived and worked on farms without electricity or mail delivery. Few people had ever heard a radio or spoken on a telephone. A hundred years later, 98 percent of American homes have telephones and televisions and more than 50 percent have personal computers. Some families even have more than one television and computer, and cell phones are now commonplace, even among the young. Data beamed from communication satellites routinely predict global weather conditions, and fiber-optic cable, e-mail, and the Internet have made worldwide telecommunication instantaneous.

Perhaps the most striking measure of scientific and technological change can be seen in medicine and public health. At the beginning of the twentieth century, the average American life span was forty-seven years. By the end of the century the average life span was approaching eighty years, thanks to advances in medicine including the development of vaccines and antibiotics, the discovery of powerful diagnostic tools such as X rays, the lifesaving technology of cardiac and neonatal care, improvements in nutrition, and the control of infectious disease.

Rapid change is likely to continue throughout the twenty-first century as science reveals more about physical and biological processes such as global warming, viral replication, and electrical conductivity, and as people apply that new knowledge to personal decisions and government policy. Already, for example, an international treaty calls for immediate reductions in industrial and automobile emissions in response to studies that show a potentially dangerous rise in global temperatures is caused by human activity. Taking an active role in determining the direction of future changes depends on education; people must understand the possible uses of scientific research and the effects of the technology that surrounds them.

The Lucent Books Library of Science and Technology profiles key innovations and discoveries that have transformed the modern world. Each title strives to make a complex scientific discovery, technology, or phenomenon understandable and relevant to the reader. Because scientific discovery is rarely straightforward, each title explains the dead ends, fortunate accidents, and basic scientific methods by which the research into the subject proceeded. And every book examines the practical applications of an invention, branch of science, or scientific principle in industry, public health, and personal life, as well as potential future uses and effects based on ongoing research. Fully documented quotations, annotated bibliographies that include both print and electronic sources, glossaries, indexes, and technical illustrations are among the supplemental features designed to point researchers to further exploration of the subject.

The World on a Desktop

Today, the word *Internet* is nearly as common as the word *telephone*. Throughout the world, people use the Internet for everything from sending e-mails to paying their bills, from shopping to getting a college education, or even casting their votes in a national election. The Internet has changed the way people communicate with each other, run their businesses, and stay informed about up-to-the-minute news events. It has also become a main source of entertainment and leisure, providing access to interactive games, electronic books (e-books), online magazines, children's activities, chat rooms—even entire museum collections. Quite simply, the Internet has become a way of life.

Medium of Mystery

Yet even though the Internet is used by millions of people all over the world, many of them do not really know what it is. They know it provides them with online access twenty-four hours a day, 7 days a week, 365 days a year. They know it allows them to do things they could not do without it. They know it simplifies their lives, and they know they get frustrated whenever it stops working. But when asked the question, "Exactly what *is* the Internet?" people are often unsure how to answer.

Every day, hundreds of millions of people all over the world, like these university students in Germany, access the massive communications network known as the Internet.

Jennifer Rasmussen, a technical writer from Virginia, worked in a university computer lab in the early 1990s. She and her staff were constantly asked questions about the Internet from novices, and she shares one particular situation:

This is one that really stands out in my mind. It was from a student who wandered into our lab looking confused, and asking, "Um, where's the Internet?" A computer tech who worked for me got this huge grin on his face, and then answered: "Well, it's like this. Looking for the

Internet is kind of like looking for God. You can go to church, you can go out into the forest, you can access God and maybe you can even *experience* God, but no matter how hard or how long you search, you're never actually going to FIND God."[1]

A Network of Networks

Although most people today are savvy enough to know the Internet is not something that can be "found," many still think it is somewhat mysterious. Some may imagine it as one gigantic supercomputer that other computers plug into, while others may think it is a building, a cluster of buildings, or some sort of official organization. Actually, the Internet is none of those things. It is a worldwide collection of computers and the enormous mass of wires and fiber-optic cables and satellite links that tie those computers together. In much the same way as personal computers (PCs) in an office building are connected through a network, the Internet ties thousands of computers and computer networks together from all over the world—which is why it is defined as a massive network of networks.

No one knows for sure exactly how many people are on the Internet. But what is known is that the number continues to increase every day. From the time the first electronic message was transmitted in 1969, the Internet has grown faster than any other technology in history. According to the U.S. Department of Commerce report "The Emerging Digital Economy," radio existed for nearly forty years before its audience reached 50 million, and it took thirteen years for television to attract that many viewers. The report states that "sixteen years after the first PC kit came out, 50 million people were using one. Once it was opened to the general public, the Internet crossed that line in four years."[2] In December 1996 the Internet's worldwide audience

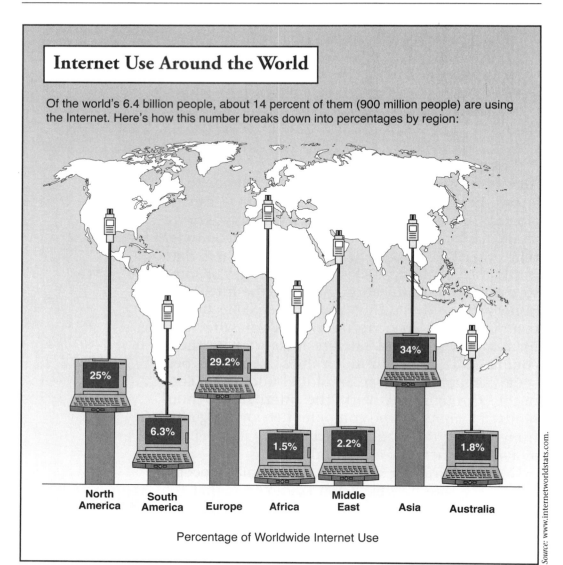

Internet Use Around the World

Of the world's 6.4 billion people, about 14 percent of them (900 million people) are using the Internet. Here's how this number breaks down into percentages by region:

25% — North America
6.3% — South America
29.2% — Europe
1.5% — Africa
2.2% — Middle East
34% — Asia
1.8% — Australia

Percentage of Worldwide Internet Use

Source: www.internetworldstats.com.

totaled about 55 million. That number had been just 16 million one year before. In only twelve months the Internet had grown by more than 325 percent.

Over the past decade the Internet has continued its astronomical growth trend. Internet World Stats estimates that nearly 900 million people worldwide were connected to the Internet as of March 2005, and the research group expects the number of users to climb to 1 billion by the end of 2005. The greatest amount of usage is in Asia, followed by Europe and North America, but the Internet's popularity is rapidly spreading to countries all over the world. According to the *CIA World Factbook*, there are thousands of Internet users in Middle Eastern countries such as Qatar, as well as in Iceland, the Bahamas, Barbados, Burma, Samoa, Guyana, and even the tiny Pacific island country of Kiribati.

As the Internet continues to grow and evolve, reaching more countries and greater numbers of the world's people, it will undoubtedly become even more important than it is today. It has the unique ability to connect people, no matter where they live or how many thousands of miles apart they may be. Because of this global connection, it is often said that the world is becoming a much smaller place. That is a direct result of the Internet.

Chapter 1

The Roots of the Internet

Even though today's Internet is used by everyone from preschoolers to politicians, accommodating the general public was not its original purpose. It began in the 1960s as a project assigned to the Advanced Research Projects Agency (ARPA), which was the problem-solving and research arm of the U.S. Department of Defense. None of the people who created it could possibly have known how it would evolve over time, nor did they have any way of knowing how important it would eventually become to millions of people. Their goal was to find a way to link computers together so resources could be shared among American military officials, scientists, and researchers. This was a daunting challenge for two reasons: The computers were not compatible with each other, and the people who needed access to the information were often thousands of miles apart. Still, the ARPA team was convinced the problem could be solved, and they believed a computer network would be the solution.

The Internet's Great-Grandfather
ARPA had originally been formed in the late 1950s to address American defense issues. It was a time known as the Cold War, and there was political tension and

deep-seated hostility between the United States and the former Soviet Union. After the end of World War II, each had begun building up its military in an effort to guard against attack from the other. When the Soviets launched *Sputnik*, the world's first satellite, the United States was caught off guard. Not only had the Soviets been the first to accomplish a space mission— their satellite was also perceived as a grave threat to America, as science writer Paul Raeburn explains: "It was a dazzling engineering achievement, and it was a powerful Cold War victory, raising fears in the United States that the Soviets might have the capability to strike the United States with a nuclear missile launched from Europe."[3] Almost immediately after *Sputnik*'s successful space journey, the Department of Defense created ARPA. The group's mission was to apply state-of-the-art technology to the U.S. defense

The former Soviet Union's launch of the world's first satellite, Sputnik, *in 1957 was perceived as a tremendous threat to U.S. security.*

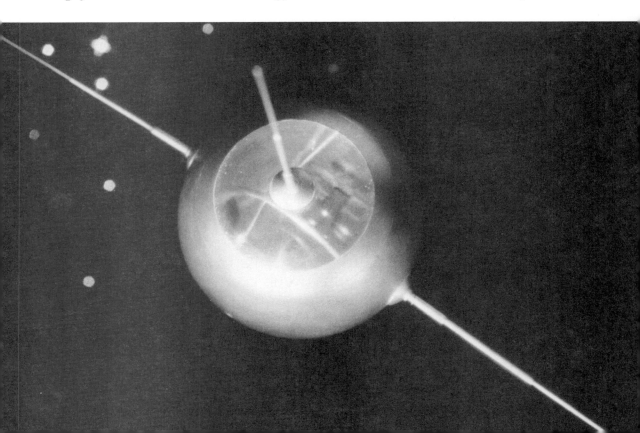

program so there would be no further surprises from adversaries such as the Soviet Union.

In 1962 ARPA formed a computer research division and appointed Joseph C.R. Licklider, a professor at the Massachusetts Institute of Technology (MIT), as its director. Licklider was known for his futuristic vision of a huge computer network that would span the globe, a system that was more powerful than anything one organization could ever build. He had written a series of memos that describe such a network, and he prophetically addressed his staff as "Members and Affiliates of the Intergalactic Computer Network." In one 1960 memo entitled "Man-Computer Symbiosis," Licklider describes his concept as follows:

> It seems reasonable to envision, for a time 10 or 15 years hence, a 'thinking center' that will incorporate the functions of present-day libraries together with anticipated advances in information storage and retrieval. . . . The picture readily enlarges itself into a network of such centers, connected to one another by wide-band communication lines and to individual users by leased-wire services.[4]

Another of Licklider's papers, which was cowritten with fellow scientist Robert Taylor, describes the network's potential in even greater detail. The scientists boldly predict that in just a few years, people would be able to communicate more effectively through computers than they could face to face. The paper describes a virtual world in which users (whom the authors referred to as "netizens") would all contribute information, as well as receive it. The result would be a vast collection of data that would be extremely useful as it continued to grow.

Other scientists shared this vision of a global network. By 1967 researchers from ARPA and MIT had developed a plan for what they called the ARPA Network, or ARPANET. It would be a system that allowed computers from remote locations to contact each other through a telephone line connection. The scientists designed the network without any central point or command center, because such a home base would make the entire network vulnerable to damage or destruction. Instead, all the computer terminals (called hosts, or nodes) would have the ability to originate, transmit, and receive their own messages. Even though they were different types of computers, they would be compatible with each other because of a set of rules and instructions known as protocols. These are to computers what language is to humans. Protocols would make it possible for computers to access each other's files and programs, so scientists and researchers could exchange valuable data even if they were located far apart.

One of the most unique features of ARPANET was the way it was designed to transmit data over the telephone lines. To send communication from one place to another, the information would be broken down into small chunks called packets. Each packet would perform like a tiny digital postcard that was individually marked with the address of its destination, as well as its originating address (like the return address on regular postal mail). The packets would wind their way through the network independently of each other, without any predetermined routes. Once they all arrived at their destination, the receiving computer would use its own software to reassemble the packets into the original file. This technology, known as packet switching, had been developed by MIT scientist Leonard Kleinrock, and it was useful because small bits of information would travel much more quickly and efficiently than huge data files.

Unlike telephone conversations, which tie up a line as long as people have the phone off the hook, packet-switching would allow lines to be in use only

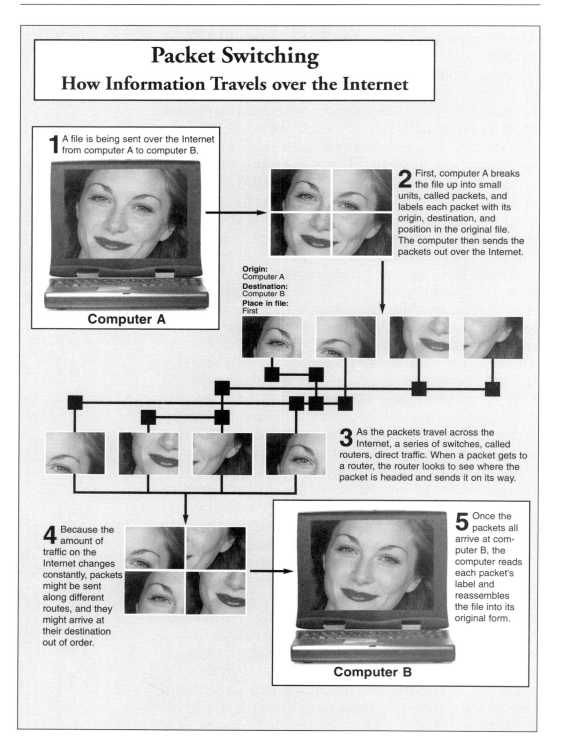

Packet Switching
How Information Travels over the Internet

1 A file is being sent over the Internet from computer A to computer B.

Computer A

2 First, computer A breaks the file up into small units, called packets, and labels each packet with its origin, destination, and position in the original file. The computer then sends the packets out over the Internet.

Origin:
Computer A
Destination:
Computer B
Place in file:
First

3 As the packets travel across the Internet, a series of switches, called routers, direct traffic. When a packet gets to a router, the router looks to see where the packet is headed and sends it on its way.

4 Because the amount of traffic on the Internet changes constantly, packets might be sent along different routes, and they might arrive at their destination out of order.

5 Once the packets all arrive at computer B, the computer reads each packet's label and reassembles the file into its original form.

Computer B

when data is actually being sent. Also, breaking messages into packets would provide greater security against eavesdroppers who might try to intercept the communication along the way. In his article, "Short History of the Internet," Bruce Sterling explains how ARPANET's packet switching worked: "The particular route that the packet took would be unimportant. Only final results would count. Basically, the packet would be tossed like a hot potato from node to node to node, more or less in the direction of its destination, until it ended up in the proper place. . . . This rather haphazard delivery system . . . would be extremely rugged."[5]

The First Critical Test

After several years of design and development, ARPANET was finally ready to be tested. The trial run took place the evening of October 29, 1969, at the University of California at Los Angeles (UCLA), and it was supervised by Kleinrock, who had joined UCLA as a professor. A computer in his laboratory was connected to a computer at the Stanford Research Institute (SRI) in Menlo Park, California, which was nearly 400 miles (644km) away. Tech students at both locations wore headsets so they could talk to each other on the telephone as they transmitted messages via computer. The plan was for Kleinrock's assistant, Charley Kline, to gain access to the SRI host by typing the word "LOGIN." Kline sat in front of the terminal and typed the letter *L*. After confirming with SRI that it had gone through, he typed an *O* and also verified that it had been received. So far, everything seemed to be going as planned—until Kline typed the letter *G*, and the entire computer system crashed. About an hour later Kleinrock's group again attempted the connection with SRI, and this time it worked. The first network test was declared a rousing success, and ARPANET was up and running.

By December 1969 two more computers had been added to the network: one at the University of California at Santa Barbara, and one at the University of Utah. Now there were four host computers, and scientists, researchers, and academicians could share information in a way that had never been possible before. Soon, additional computers began connecting to ARPANET. By late 1972 twenty-four host computers were linked to each other through the network. These included the four original hosts as well as computers at MIT and Harvard, the U.S. Department of Defense, the National Science Foundation, the Federal Reserve Board, and the National Aeronautics and Space Administration (NASA).

Communicating Electronically

In addition to ARPANET's information-sharing ability, there was another reason it was becoming so popular: It could be used for electronic mail. Before the network existed, e-mail could only be transmitted through "local" message programs, which had limited capabilities: People could only exchange messages if they logged onto the same computer at different times. One of these programs, called SNDMSG, had been developed by a computer engineer named Ray Tomlinson. Once ARPANET was functioning, Tomlinson refined his program so it was capable of sending electronic messages between different computers on the network. In 1971 Tomlinson tested his program by sending a message from one computer to another that was sitting next to it. The e-mail simply read "QWERTYUIOP," the first line of letters on a standard keyboard. However, it was one of the most important developments in technological history because it ushered in the era of electronic network mail.

After Tomlinson's test message worked as planned, he sent an e-mail to all ARPANET users, announcing the capabilities of SNDMSG. His note included in-

Pictures over Wires

Today, people who use the Internet are able to view everything from photographs to streaming video. This is an example of highly sophisticated technology that has only become available in recent years, but the concept of transmitting pictures over wires was actually born long before ARPANET ever existed. In 1956 a combination telephone and television system called the Picturephone was developed by Bell Laboratories, and it was advertised to consumers with the slogan, "Someday you'll be a star!"

The Picturephone was presented at the 1964 New York World's Fair, where people were able to actually use it. The product was hailed by its creators as the wave of the future—but the public did not agree. They felt it was too bulky, with controls that were difficult to understand. They also complained that it was harder to use than a regular telephone, the picture was too small, and they did not like the idea of having others see them while they talked on the phone.

Over the following years there were more attempts to market the Picturephone, but none were successful. The project was eventually scrapped, and it came to be known as one of the worst communication flops in history.

In 1965 a young woman smiles as the image of the person she is communicating with appears on the Picturephone screen.

structions for how to properly address e-mail to others in the network, using the "@" symbol between the user's log-in name and the name of his or her host computer. When people became aware that they could use e-mail, it quickly became a popular way of communicating, as Sterling explains:

> ARPANET's users had warped the computer-sharing network into a dedicated, high-speed, federally subsidized electronic post office. The main traffic on ARPANET was not long-distance computing. Instead, it was news and personal messages. Researchers were using ARPANET to collaborate on projects, to trade notes on work, and eventually, to downright gossip and schmooze.[6]

Before long, another type of electronic communication, known as the mailing list, was created. Mailing lists were in the form of e-mails, but they were intended to be sent to large numbers of ARPANET users all at once. Some of the most popular early mailing lists were *Network-Hackers*, which dealt with programming and other technical issues; *SF-Lovers*, designed especially for science fiction fans; *Wine-Tasters*, for people who fancied themselves as wine connoisseurs; and *Human-Nets*, a forum for discussing the relationship between humans and technology.

Growing Pains

Because of ARPANET's ability to facilitate information sharing, as well as how it supported electronic communication, excitement over the network began to build. However, it was still relatively unknown because the news had not been made public. In October 1972 ARPA scientists made a formal presentation at the International Conference on Computers and Communication, which was held in Washington, D.C. Their audience included representatives from France, Japan, Norway, Sweden, Great Britain, and Canada, as well as the United States. Attendees were extremely impressed with the demonstration, as well as being excited about ARPANET'S tremendous potential.

Once the public became aware of ARPANET and its capabilities, more and more computers began connecting to it. By the end of 1973 the number of ARPANET hosts had grown to thirty-seven, and a satellite link had been made between California and Hawaii. Also in 1973, the first international connections were made when England's University College of London and Norway's Royal Radar Establishment became part of the network. Soon, entire computer networks started hooking into ARPANET as well— and along with them came a whole new set of problems. Each of the networks had its own unique design, as well as its own way of transmitting packets, and these differences caused a serious language barrier. Suddenly, many computers within ARPANET were not compatible with each other and could not exchange information, which meant the original protocols were no longer adequate. New protocols were needed that were capable of linking not only computers but also entire networks together in one interconnected system.

Computer scientists Vinton Cerf and Bob Kahn, both of whom were part of the ARPANET team, began designing the new protocols in 1973. Their work on what they called "Internetting Project" took nearly five years, and the result was a vastly improved set of protocols called the transmission-control protocol/Internet protocol (TCP/IP) suite. In an online biography of Cerf, MIT describes how the new system worked: "Simply stated, TCP/IP allows for the 'handshake' that introduces distant and different computers to each other in a virtual space. TCP controls and keeps track of the flow of data packets; IP addresses and forwards individual packets."[7] By 1978,

In 1973 computer scientist Vinton Cerf (left) and Bob Kahn began designing protocols to link computer networks across the world in one interconnected system.

an expanding group of networks had begun using TCP/IP to link to ARPANET. Cerf later wrote a paper that referred to the connected system of networks as "the Internet."

Continued Evolution

With the creation of TCP/IP, ARPANET had become more functional than ever before. During the late 1970s the number of hosts and networks connected to it continued to increase, and it was growing larger every day. Also, numerous government organizations, scientific groups, and educational institutions began developing their own independent networks, which they connected to ARPANET. However, participation was not limited to these types of groups. The network was completely public, available to anyone who had access to the software and could figure out how to connect. Sterling describes the ease of joining:

> It was difficult to stop people from barging in and linking up somewhere-or-other. In point of fact, nobody wanted to stop them from joining this branching complex of networks, which

came to be known as the "Internet."... The more the merrier. Like the phone network, the computer network became steadily more valuable as it embraced larger and larger territories of people and resources.[8]

As of March 1977 there were a total of 111 hosts and a number of individual networks connected to ARPANET. And while it remained the backbone of the system, it was becoming smaller and smaller as it was engulfed by the enormous maze of computers and networks linking to it.

In 1979 a new type of network was conceived by two Duke University graduate students named Tom Truscott and Jim Ellis. They were interested in starting ongoing electronic discussions that dealt with technical issues, and neither electronic mail nor mailing lists could achieve what they had in mind. They conferred with Steve Bellovin, an acquaintance who attended the University of North Carolina, about their idea. Bellovin developed software for an online discussion forum, and the two universities were soon connected. The program, which was named Usenet, allowed about a dozen text messages (called "articles") to be transferred between the two universities' computers each day.

In the beginning Usenet was just a small network where a handful of students chatted about computer-related issues. Its popularity spread quickly, though, and many other discussion forums (known as newsgroups) began to spring up. In addition to technical categories, there were also discussions about topics such as science fiction, literature, music, and comedy. Based on their interests, people could subscribe to newsgroups and download the ongoing dialogues to their computers. Then they could post their own opinions about a topic or start a new discussion "thread" as well as ask for advice, enter into debates about controversial issues, and develop virtual relationships

The Internet Myth

It is a popular belief that ARPANET was originally built to be tough enough to survive anything—even a nuclear war. Numerous information sources, including Web sites that focus on Internet history, present this as if it were a fact—but although it makes a good story, it is nothing more than a myth. In an article on the Web site About.com Charles Herzfeld, who was director of ARPA when the network was first conceived, tells what actually happened.

> Most of the early "history" on the subject is wrong. . . . The ARPAnet was not started to create a Command and Control System that would survive a nuclear attack, as many now claim. To build such a system was clearly a major military need, but it was not ARPA's mission to do this; in fact, we would have been severely criticized had we tried. Rather, the ARPAnet came out of our frustration that there were only a limited number of large, powerful research computers in the country, and that many research investigators who should have access to them were geographically separated from them. . . . [The ARPANET team] wanted to see if there was a way to link the computers to each other, and connect the users to these netted computers in a way that facilitated access by the researchers. At the time, no one knew whether this could be done at all, so the program was clearly a high-risk one. The potential military applications (including the potential for robust communications) were well in our minds, but they were not our primary responsibility

with people of similar interests. Within a few years of Usenet's creation, several other universities and organizations had begun to participate, and the software was revised to accommodate this growth. Eventually, the Usenet software was redesigned so it could run not only as an independent network, but also on ARPANET.

Amazing Growth

In the 1980s ARPANET's growth began to skyrocket, and it took on the name that had been coined by Cerf: the Internet. By 1984 there were over a thousand hosts, and this burgeoning network of networks was growing at a rate of speed that no one could ever have imagined. In fact, it was expanding so fast that some people predicted the whole thing was surely headed for a massive collapse.

One important development during the 1980s was the creation of the domain name system (DNS), which was designed by Paul Mockapetris of the University of Southern California's Information Science Institute. Prior to DNS, all host computers were assigned the same identification: HOSTS.TXT. This worked fine when the network was composed of just a few hundred computers, but as its population began to explode, a new system was sorely needed. The DNS introduced a series of special codes (a form of tiering system) that identifies the different varieties of hosts and keeps them separate from each other. Hosts from other countries are denoted by their geographical locations, while those within the United States are identified based on what type of organizations they are. Domains are indicated by suffixes such as .com (pronounced "dot com") for commercial establishments; .org for nonprofit organizations; .gov for federal government agencies; .mil for any department or agency of the military; and .edu for educational institutions. The .net suffix designates computers that are "gateways" between the individual networks, such as Internet service providers (ISPs).

Throughout the rest of the 1980s the Internet continued to grow—and grow—and grow. By 1986 there were more than five thousand hosts, and one year later it had climbed to an astounding twenty-eight thousand. When the number reached three hundred thousand in 1990, it was determined that the original ARPANET had outlived its usefulness and it was retired. What had started as a tiny network connecting two university computers a few hundred miles apart had morphed into a massive network of networks that spans the entire globe. Yet even though the Internet had grown beyond anyone's wildest imagination, there was still no end in sight.

Chapter 2

Enter the World Wide Web

Even as the Internet's growth continued its up-ward spiral, it was still mysterious and difficult to understand. Only the most astute programmers (often called "computer geeks" or "techies") knew how to navigate through the complicated maze in order to use its resources. For one thing, even though there were hundreds of thousands of host computers connected to the Internet, there was no way to search for them. If a user was lucky enough to run across an excellent source of information, there was no way to bookmark its location. In order to return to particular sites, people had to write down the numerical addresses and build their own lists. The computer mouse was still not a common accessory, so users could not simply "point and click." Instead, they had to manually type in long strings of numbers (or commands) every time they wanted to gain access to a site. In addition, every computer that was connected to the Internet had its own unique password. So, along with compiling extensive lists of host sites, users also had to keep track of all the different passwords.

Even making a connection with another computer did not guarantee that files could be accessed because getting at the data was far from easy. After navigating through a complicated maze of technical-sounding terms, a user had to type in the commands in precisely the right order. If even one symbol were typed incorrectly—such as a semicolon instead of a period, or a number sign instead of an asterisk—the host computer would not respond. Finding information on the Internet was so tedious and difficult that many people grew frustrated very quickly.

A "Magical Doorway"

Tim Berners-Lee, a computer consultant with a research organization in Switzerland called CERN, believed there had to be a way of simplifying the Internet. Berners-Lee himself had a great deal of technical knowledge, but he was convinced that if the Internet was easier to use, its vast store of information would become more valuable than ever. He

Tim Berners-Lee devised software that made the information on the Internet accessible to people across the globe. He named his creation the World Wide Web.

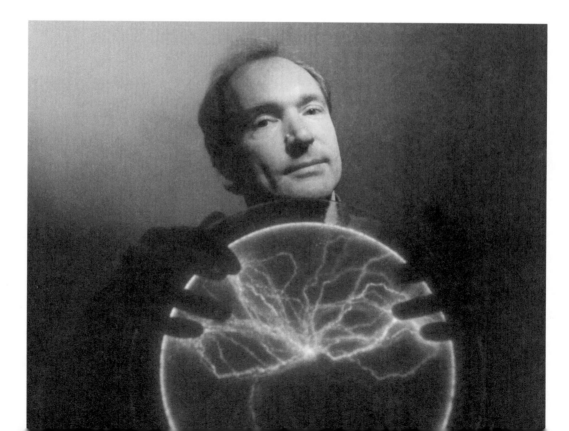

often found himself imagining the possibilities: *"Suppose all the information stored on computers everywhere were linked*, I thought. *Suppose I could program my computer to create a space in which anything could be linked to anything.* All the bits of information in every computer at CERN, and on the planet, would be available to me and to anyone else. There would be a single, global information space."[9]

Berners-Lee had always loved anything related to electronics. As a child he had built pretend computers out of cardboard boxes, and when he was attending Oxford University, he had built a real working computer out of spare parts and an old television. In 1980 he wrote a software program in his spare time and named it Enquire. The name was taken from the title of a book, *Enquire Within upon Everything*, which had fascinated him when he was young. He later referred to it as "a musty old book of Victorian advice," but his childhood impression was that it was a magical doorway to the wealth of information contained in the book. He was enticed by the title page, which immodestly claimed: "Whether you wish to model a flower in wax; to study the rules of etiquette; to serve relish for breakfast or supper; to plan a dinner for a large party or a small one; to cure a headache; to make a will; to get married; to bury a relative; whatever you may wish to do, make, or to enjoy, provided your desire has relation to the necessities of domestic life, I hope you will not fail to 'Enquire Within.'"[10]

Berners-Lee originally created Enquire for his own personal use at CERN. The organization was enormous, with sprawling buildings, thousands of people, and hundreds of computer systems. Enquire allowed him to keep track of all the different projects, the people who were assigned to the projects, what computers were used, what types of programs there were, and who had written the programs.

One of Enquire's components was a tool that allowed certain pages and words to be linked to other

The Internet Gopher

Before the days of search engines, before the Web, before there was much semblance of order or organization on the Internet, there was something called Gopher. The program, which provided users with a menu of viewable text-based files, was developed by college students Paul Lindner and Mark P. McCahill, who named it after the University of Minnesota's Golden Gophers sports teams.

The Gopher system was based on several hundred servers and thousands of Gopher clients, or computers that retrieved information from the servers. It featured two search tools named Veronica and Archie, after the famous comic book characters. Veronica, which was known as an indexing spider, allowed users to search files on a server for a particular string of text. Veronica could visit Internet sites, read all the directory and file names, and then store them in a large index. Archie was also an early form of search engine, but it was used to search other types of files.

Compared to today's slick, speedy search engines, Gopher is a simple, basic tool. Although it is still used by some government agencies and universities, its use has been almost entirely surpassed by the Web. To some people it may even seem like an antique—but for people who muddled their way through the Internet in the early days, Gopher was a product that made their efforts a lot simpler.

files on Berners-Lee's computer—similar to the links in a chain. He modeled the function after a concept known as hypertext, which had been introduced by computer scientists in the 1960s. Hypertext was a unique system that enabled links to connect documents and programs on one computer, as well as between separate computers. By following these hyperlinks, Berners-Lee could easily move from one area to another in any order he chose.

Even though he had developed Enquire exclusively for himself, he was certain it had much greater potential. But about the time he was starting to refine it, his consulting job with CERN ended. When he left the organization he saved the program on a disk and gave it to one of the employees, in case someone might be able to use it. No one did, though, and eventually, the disk—containing the only copy of Enquire—was lost.

Lofty Dreams

After a few years at another company, Berners-Lee returned to CERN in 1984. Once again he needed special software for his job, and he decided to re-create Enquire from scratch. He explains why:

> In addition to keeping track of relationships between all the people, experiments, and machines, I wanted to access different kinds of information, such as a researcher's technical papers, the manuals for different software modules, minutes of meetings, hastily scribbled notes, and so on. Furthermore, I found myself answering the same questions asked frequently of me by different people. It would be so much easier if everyone could just read my database.[11]

As before, Berners-Lee had much bigger dreams for his software. He began to think about how it could benefit people throughout the CERN organization—but an even loftier goal was to make it available to users of the Internet, so information would be accessible to people all over the world. In the same way he had viewed the title *Enquire Within upon Anything* as a magical doorway into a book's vast store of knowledge, he believed his software program could serve as a magical doorway into the Internet.

Berners-Lee was convinced that hypertext was the secret to creating the global system he had envisioned for many years:

> An Enquire program capable of external hypertext links was the difference between imprisonment and freedom, dark and light. New webs could be made to bind different computers together, and all new systems would be able to break out and reference others. Plus, anyone browsing could instantly add a new node connected by a new link. . . . I wanted the act of

adding a new link to be trivial; if it was, then a web of links could spread evenly across the globe.[12]

As confident as Berners-Lee was in his visionary idea, there was much work to be done. He knew that such an aggressive project would be complicated as well as expensive, and he had no tangible proof that it could actually work. Fortunately, another computer scientist named Robert Cailliau shared his enthusiasm. He had previously proposed developing his own hypertext system at CERN, and he partnered with Berners-Lee to generate corporate support and funding for the new project. One decision they made was that the software would need a new name—one that did a better job of communicating its usefulness as a global tool. After considering such options as "Information Mesh," "Mine of Information," and "The Information Mine," Berners-Lee finally chose a name he felt was most suitable: the World Wide Web.

In September 1990 he and Cailliau traveled to Versailles, France, to attend the European Conference on Hypertext. There were a number of products on display, one of which was a hypertext program called Guide. Berners-Lee was very interested in it because it looked almost exactly like what he had envisioned for a Web browser, the program that would open and display documents on users' computer screens. He talked with Guide's developers about the vast potential if such a program were used on the Internet, but he could not convince them. He describes the typical reaction: "It seemed that explaining the vision of the Web to people was exceedingly difficult without a Web browser in hand. People had to be able to grasp the Web in full, which meant imagining a whole world populated with Web sites and browsers. They had to sense the abstract information space that the Web could bring into being. It was a lot to ask."[13] Steadfast in his belief of the Web's potential, Berners-Lee left the conference with a new goal: He would develop the software on his own, including a browser, just as he had created Enquire.

Spinning the Web

Back at CERN, Berners-Lee was given a new desktop computer with features such as a mouse and hypertext software—highly advanced technology for the time. He was also given the green flag from his supervisor to start working on the global hypertext system. His first task was to write the Web "client," or the root program that would allow him to create, browse, and edit hypertext pages. Once that was completed, he developed a method of converting plain text into hypertext so links could be created within documents. He then wrote the hypertext transfer protocol

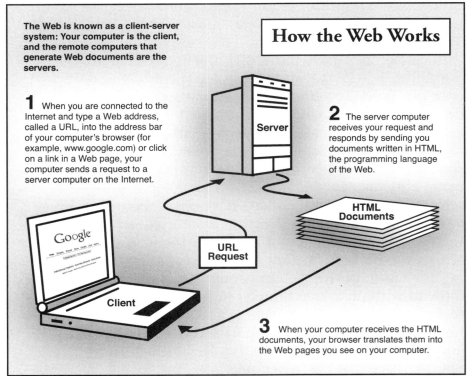

The Web is known as a client-server system: Your computer is the client, and the remote computers that generate Web documents are the servers.

How the Web Works

1 When you are connected to the Internet and type a Web address, called a URL, into the address bar of your computer's browser (for example, www.google.com) or click on a link in a Web page, your computer sends a request to a server computer on the Internet.

2 The server computer receives your request and responds by sending you documents written in HTML, the programming language of the Web.

Server

HTML Documents

URL Request

Google

Client

3 When your computer receives the HTML documents, your browser translates them into the Web pages you see on your computer.

Source: CERN 2005—Web Communications, http://public.web.cem.ch/Public/Welcome.html.

(HTTP), a programming language that would allow Web pages to be linked together on computers across the Internet. He also developed a method of assigning Web sites their own unique addresses, which he called the universal resource identifier, or URI (later named uniform resource locater, or URL). Next, he created a system known as the hypertext markup language (HTML) that describes how to format pages containing hypertext links. It was HTML that would allow links to remain hidden within Web pages, as well as provide access to other places within a Web site and to other sites on the Internet.

By the winter of 1990 Berners-Lee had finished developing the program, which featured a point-and-click browser that he named the WorldWideWeb. (He later changed the name so the browser would not be confused with the global information space called the World Wide Web.) He also developed the world's first Web server, or a program that allows Web documents stored on one computer to be accessed by other computers. He explains his creation and how it was designed to function on the Internet:

> The Web is an abstract (imaginary) space of information. On the Net, you find computers—on the Web, you find document[s], sounds, videos . . . information. On the Net, the connections are cables between computers; on the Web, connections are hypertext links. The Web exists because of programs which communicate between computers on the Net. The Web could not be without the Net. The Web made the Net useful because people are really interested in information (not to mention knowledge and wisdom!) and don't really want to have to know about computers and cables.[14]

The highlight of Berners-Lee's efforts was seeing his program in action for the first time. He installed it on Cailliau's computer, and on December 25, 1990, the two were sharing hypertext documents between their machines. After that, they began demonstrating the Web to colleagues at CERN, and they received mixed reactions; some people were positive, while others were neutral or even pessimistic. Berners-Lee found that many of them still did not realize how powerful the Web could be, nor did they share his vision for its great potential. This was partly because they expected the program to be much more complicated than it actually was, as he explains:

> What was often difficult for people to understand about the design was that there was nothing else beyond URIs, HTTP, and HTML. There was no central computer "controlling" the Web, no single network on which these protocols worked, not even an organization anywhere that "ran" the Web. The Web was not a physical "thing" that existed in a certain "place." It was a "space" in which information could exist.[15]

The News Begins to Spread

Berners-Lee continued to demonstrate his Web program as often as possible. He wanted to spread the word outside of CERN, so during August 1991 he announced it on four different Internet newsgroups. One was *alt.hypertext*, which was frequented by computer programmers who were interested in hypertext technology. Berners-Lee's post states that the Web project "merges the techniques of information retrieval and hypertext to make an easy but powerful global information system."[16] He explains what the program is, how it works, and why it is so exciting. He also gives information about where to download the browser for free. He did not want to charge for it because he strongly believed that the Web could succeed only if no one owned or controlled it.

In September 1991 an American named Paul Kunz traveled to Switzerland to see a demonstration of the new software. Kunz was a physicist with the Stanford Linear Accelerator Center (SLAC) in Stanford, California. He became very excited about the Web's potential, and when he left CERN to return to the United States, he took a copy of Berners-Lee's software with him. By December he and one of his associates had set up a Web server at SLAC—the first Web server to be installed outside of Europe. One month later, at a workshop on advanced computing techniques that was held in France, Berners-Lee demonstrated his Web program to two hundred scientists from around the world. As a grand finale, he used his computer and browser to connect to a database located 6,000 miles (9,656km) away at SLAC. Kunz describes the group's reaction:

In 1991 physicist Paul Kunz installed a Web server at Stanford University, the first server to be set up outside Europe.

This opened people's eyes. Their jaws just dropped. They knew the database, and they saw how easy it was to access it from this town in southern France. You had these 200 people, who were coming from maybe 100 or more different institutes from around the world, and imagine how anxious they were to get back home and show their colleagues! That was a giant push in advancing the Web.[17]

Meteoric Growth

News of the ingenious new system began to spread rapidly, and Web sites started popping up around the world. In 1993, two years after Berners-Lee announced the software and made it available, there were 130 sites on the Web, and the number was doubling every three months. One reason the Web was becoming so popular is because new browsers were being developed that made it compatible with more types of computers as well as easier for people to use. One of these browsers was called Mosaic, which was introduced in 1993. It was created by Marc Andreessen, a student at the University of Illinois, and Eric Bina, a programmer at the university's National Center for Supercomputing Applications. Mosaic became known as the "killer application" of the 1990s, because people found it so useful that they bought computers just for the sake of running it. In 1995, Andreessen became a cofounder of a company known as Netscape Communications, and Mosaic's name was changed to Netscape Navigator. Soon, other developers began creating browsers, such as Microsoft's Internet Explorer, which was first introduced in 1995. At that point, the Web began to grow at lightning-fast speed.

In January 1996 the number of Internet hosts had grown to 9.5 million, and there were more than one hundred thousand Web sites. One year later the number of Web sites had jumped to over six hundred thousand, and by 1998 it had surpassed 2.5 million.

The Web Today

No one is positive of how many sites currently exist on the World Wide Web because there is no way to make an exact count. According to the search engine Google, as of June 2005 there were more than 8 billion distinct Web pages. Web sites are made up of multiple pages, so how that number translates into the total number of sites becomes an educated guess.

Web Medicine

Even though people often think of the Web as something that makes their lives easier, they may not think about its potential to save lives. Yet that is exactly the goal of NASA's Virtual Collaborative Clinic, a high-speed satellite-linked network that connects medical facilities around the United States. By using the virtual clinic, doctors at world-class medical centers are able to diagnose patients and consult with other physicians via computer. Using this kind of virtual technology, local hospitals can access resources and skills that are only available at much larger health care institutions.

This type of technology could mean the difference between life and death for patients who require specialized medical treatment. For instance, in 1998 a baby girl named Morgan Kaupp was born with a serious heart problem. An ultrasound exam revealed that a hole was leaking blood between her heart's two main chambers. There was no cardiologist on staff and Morgan's doctors were not sure whether to operate, so they made a videocassette copy of the ultrasound images and sent it via courier to a heart specialist. Morgan's heart eventually healed on its own—but her life was at risk while the seconds ticked away. The Virtual Collaborative Clinic could make such practices obsolete because doctors and specialists will be able to confer instantaneously on the Internet.

Physicians can also use the Virtual Collaborative Clinic to practice surgery by using a virtual reality tool called CyberScalpel. This technology allows surgeons to "operate" on three-dimensional images on a computer screen, so they can test or rehearse procedures before operating on a patient. Another of NASA's goals is to use the program to provide remote health care to astronauts on extended space journeys. For instance, if an astronaut were to suffer a fractured leg, members of a virtual clinic on Earth could use CyberScalpel to reconstruct the fracture and display the steps needed to repair it. Then, images from the virtual operation could be transmitted to the nonphysician caregivers in space, who could use it as a guide during the actual procedure.

Assuming that the average Web site is composed of fifty pages, that would mean there were about 160 million sites on the Web—but many experts claim the number is much higher.

Today, the World Wide Web looks nothing like the system that Berners-Lee envisioned back in the 1980s, when he used hypertext to create Enquire. Today's Web is slick, colorful, musical, and interactive, with capabilities that continue to grow more and more sophisticated every day. Yet even though the exact numbers are not known, what is certain is that the Web continues to constantly grow and change. Berners-Lee offers his perspective on the dream that became a reality:

> I was very lucky, in working at CERN, to be in an environment . . . of mutual respect, and of building something very great through collective effort that was well beyond the means of any one person. . . . This system produced a weird and wonderful machine, which needed care to maintain, but could take advantage of the ingenuity, inspiration, and intuition of individuals in a special way. That, from the start, has been my goal for the World Wide Web.[18]

Chapter 3

How the Internet Works

Since ARPANET was first introduced in the 1960s, the Internet has grown from four host computers at two California universities to millions of host computers all over the world. Even though futuristic scientists envisioned some sort of worldwide network when they created it, there was no "master plan" for how the Internet would eventually look. In fact, its form and structure have just continued to evolve over the years as it has grown, and this has created a system that is highly complex. In his book, *The Complete Idiot's Guide to the Internet*, author Peter Kent uses an analogy to describe the Internet's complexity:

> The problem . . . lies in the way it has come to be. It's a problem of planning, and it's an inevitable result of the way the network grew. As an example of this theory, compare the cities of Dallas and London. London is a confusing mesh of intertwining roads, while Dallas is laid out on a sensible grid system. London wasn't planned, it just grew. Dallas was planned almost right from the start. The Internet wasn't developed as a single planned system. It just grew. . . . Going out alone into Internet-land is like venturing on

39

The Structure of the Internet

1 The Internet lets people exchange information on computers in homes, businesses, universities, and government agencies.

2 Every computer is equipped with a modem or another device for sending and receiving digitized information (words, pictures, sound) over the Internet.

3 Satellites, phone lines, and fiber optic cables relay the information that computers send and receive.

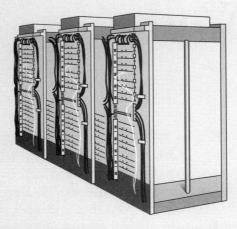

4 Internet service providers (ISPs) provide access to the powerful computing and switching equipment that forms the backbone of the Internet. This equipment is run by large companies, universities, and government agencies around the world.

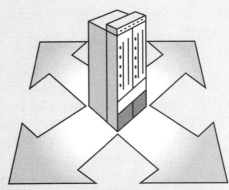

5 Routing computers direct Internet traffic. They decode instructions in the transmitted information that tell them how and where to send it.

foot across London without a guide or map. It'll be interesting, but you may not find what you're looking for.[19]

The Infrastructure

As complex and free-flowing as the Internet is, the matrix of networks it comprises forms a distinct framework known as an infrastructure. It is like the branches of a massive tree, stretching out in all directions and spanning the entire planet. To fully understand this interconnected system, it is necessary to examine the different types of networks and how they perform. After all, those networks *are* the Internet—even its very name comes from the global collection of *inter*connected *net*works.

The Internet's networks range from very small to enormous. The most basic type is the LAN, an acronym that stands for "local area network." LANs are used to connect computers that are located in the same home, office, or building, and they allow computer users to share information and resources such as software and common files, as well as printers and other equipment. Typically, one computer within a LAN is designated as the file server, which means its only function is to manage and control the network. The other computers are known as workstations or "clients," and are connected to each other with wires and cables or through wireless technology.

But LANs are not limited to connecting computers in the same geographic location. They are also used to connect computers located thousands of miles apart. For instance, corporations often have large internal networks known as intranets, which use fiber-optic technology or satellite links to connect branch offices located in distant states or countries. Nancy Ahern, a software engineer who lives in Arizona and works for a Chicago-based international technology company, describes how her company's intranet benefits employees:

Fiber Optics

Whenever people talk on the telephone, tune in to their favorite cable TV stations, or use the Internet, fiber optics are likely responsible for the transmission. Fiber-optic lines are strands of pure glass (or sometimes plastic) that are as thin as a human hair. The innermost region of each fiber is the core, through which light is transmitted. An outer layer of coating, known as cladding, prevents the light from leaking out of the core. The glass fibers are bundled together to make optical cables and then used to transmit light energy. Fiber optics works on the principle of bending light, which Craig C. Freudenrich, explains on the Web site HowStuffWorks:

> Suppose you want to shine a flashlight beam down a long, straight hallway. Just point the beam straight down the hallway—light travels in straight lines, so it is no problem. What if the hallway has a bend in it? You could place a mirror at the bend to reflect the light beam around the corner. What if the hallway was very winding with multiple bends? You might line the walls with mirrors and angle the beam so that it bounces from side-to-side all along the hallway. This is exactly what happens in an optical fiber. The light in a fiber-optic cable travels through the core (hallway) by constantly bouncing from the cladding (mirror-lined walls), a principle called total internal reflection. Because the cladding does not absorb any light from the core, the light wave can travel great distances.

Light travels along fiber-optic cables in the same way that electricity travels along copper wires, but fiber optics is superior for many reasons. The strands are thin and lightweight so hundreds or thousands of fibers can be bundled into a cable. As a result, a single fiber-optic cable can replace a traditional wire trunk line measuring 10 feet (3m) in diameter. The signals sent through a fiber-optic network are often digital, so humans and computers can use the same lines. Also, because light has such a high frequency, fiber-optic cables have a wider bandwidth and can carry more information at one time. And because the cables are used to transmit light instead of electricity, they are safer because there is no risk of fire.

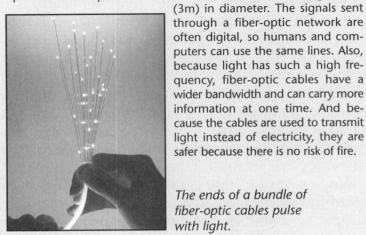

The ends of a bundle of fiber-optic cables pulse with light.

Our company is very large and has a global presence, with offices in Canada, Ireland, England, Israel, Germany, India, Singapore, China, Mexico, Venezuela, and Spain, among others. The entire company is connected through our own intranet. Even if we never connected to the outside world (the Internet), we'd still have complete electronic access to one another. We have internal e-mail, instant messaging, NetMeetings, newsgroups, and discussion forums where our technical experts can draw on the experience of others. Only those who are connected via the company's intranet can see any of this stuff, or use it. It's how we all communicate with one another, sharing information and files among people who are spread all over the world.[20]

Some of the largest and most spread-out LANs are online services such as CompuServe, America Online, and Prodigy. These entities are usually associated with the Internet because in addition to providing their own array of information, they also provide Web access. That was not always the case, however, because online services were operating years before the Web was invented. One of the earliest was called The Source, which operated from 1978 until 1989, when it was purchased by CompuServe. For an hourly fee, members of The Source could dial into the network and read the news, weather reports, and stock quotations, as well as access online shopping, electronic mail, the text of selected magazines, and airline schedules. Like corporate intranets, the Source and other online service pioneers offered goods and services exclusively to members who paid to access their networks.

The Network Hierarchy

The various types of LANs can offer users a wealth of information, but to provide access to the Internet, they need some type of Internet provider. This has only been in practice since the late 1980s. Prior to that, as long as people knew how to dial into remote computers, they could enter passwords and gain access to the information that was stored on the computers. When the Internet began its rapid growth boom, dozens of Internet service provider (ISP) businesses began forming to offer Internet access to individuals, businesses, schools, and other organizations. By the mid-1990s CompuServe and other online services were providing their subscribers with Internet access; in doing so, they also assumed the role of ISPs.

The amount of data that an ISP's network can transmit is known as bandwidth, and this can vary widely based on the size of the provider. Generally, the larger the ISP, the greater amount of bandwidth is available to customers, which makes for a faster connection. The Web site Find an ISP compares bandwidth to a water system by explaining that "the bandwidth is the limit on how much water comes out of the pipe when you open the faucet. Your connection can be slow either because your bandwidth pipe isn't big enough at some place in the system, or because there are [too] many people sharing the same 'pipe.'"[21]

Internet Backbones

There is a definite hierarchy of how ISPs connect people to the Internet. Small regional providers generally lease bandwidth from larger ISPs. The next level up is network service providers, or NSPs, which provide bandwidth to ISPs through high-speed interconnecting networks known as backbones. These backbones may be composed of fiber-optic trunk lines, satellite links, and powerful switching and computing equipment, and they provide lightning-fast connections. Today, most of the world's large communication companies have their own dedicated backbones that connect various regions. Some major worldwide backbones include the GÉANT, which connects networks in major cities throughout Europe; FORTH-net, a backbone in Greece; GARR-B, which connects the networks of scientific institutions in Italy; and Golden Telecom, located in Russia. In the United States, major backbones are owned and operated by Sprint, MCI, IBM, and WorldCom's UUNET, among others. There are also privately owned and operated backbones that provide direct Internet access through high-speed connections. Two examples of such backbones are integrated services digital network (ISDN) and T1 lines.

The first backbone was created in the mid-1980s by the National Science Foundation (NSF), whose goal was to streamline network traffic so the Internet's resources were more accessible to scientists and researchers. The NSF set up six supercomputer centers around the United States and then built a high-speed network, called NSFNET, to connect them. This was a significant development in the Internet's growth, as Bruce Sterling explains:

> The new NSFNET set a blistering pace for technical advancement, linking newer, faster, shinier supercomputers through thicker, faster links, upgraded and expanded, again and again, in 1986, 1988, 1990. And other government agencies leapt in: NASA, the National Institutes of Health, the Department of Energy, each of them maintaining a digital [territory] in the Internet confederation.[22]

By the early 1990s, other commercial networks were building their own backbone infrastructures.

All backbones interlink with each other at public network exchange facilities known as network access points (NAPs), the hubs of the Internet. These Internet hubs could be compared to major airport hubs, where planes arrive from all over the world to be rerouted toward their next destination—but unlike airports, NAPs perform their tasks at the speed of light. An article on the HowStuffWorks Web site describes the constant interconnection between networks: "In this way, everyone on the Internet, no matter where they are and what company they use, is able to talk to everyone else on the planet. The entire Internet is a gigantic, sprawling agreement between companies to intercommunicate freely."[23]

Directing Traffic

As gigantic, sprawling, and complex as the Internet is, data packets can still zoom from one side of the planet to the other—and that is one of the Internet's

A technician performs maintenance on an Internet cable router. Routers allow data to be transferred between networks.

most amazing qualities. A crucial element in its ability to maintain this constant (and enormous) flow of data is the router, a specialized behind-the-scenes computer. Routers provide bridges between networks, allowing data to flow between separate networks, rather than just inside of them. They are used when two remote LANs need to connect with each other, as well as when any network needs to connect to the Internet, and their most basic function is figuring out how and where to send data packets. This involves determining the best available connection path between networks and ensuring that the data travels along the fastest possible route. The keyword here is "fast," because the path chosen by a router may not necessarily be the shortest one.

In performing their jobs, routers have two separate —albeit related—tasks. First, they stop information from going where it is not supposed to go. This is important because it prevents traffic on one network from unnecessarily spilling over onto another, which protects "innocent bystander" connections from getting clogged with huge amounts of data. A router's second function is to make sure data *does* make it to the intended destination. Routers communicate with each other through protocols, which allow them to configure the best route between any two hosts. They can also perform translations when they find network protocols to be incompatible, and they can provide additional security for a network.

So how does a router do its work? Inside is a control mechanism known as a configuration table, which contains information that is crucial for data to travel throughout the network. Configuration tables contain such data as all the possible routes packets could take, which connections lead to particular groups of addresses, and rules for handling traffic. In small routers, configuration tables may consist of just half a dozen lines of computer programming code. In very large routers (some of which use the same design as the most powerful supercomputers in the world), the tables are often enormous as well as highly complex. Whatever their size, routers depend on these configuration tables to provide them with all the information they need to do their jobs.

Is Anyone in Charge?

Because all the routers, hubs, protocols, and backbones work together so efficiently, Internet traffic constantly moves throughout the worldwide maze of networks. And one of the most incredible things about this interconnected system is that it operates without any one person or organization owning or controlling it. There is no "Internet Incorporated," no president or vice president, no supreme ruling body. Although ISPs have their own terms of use that subscribers must abide by, the Internet itself is not governed by such rules. Using an unusual analogy, Sterling compares this lack of overall authority with the English language:

> [Nobody] owns English. As an English-speaking person, it's up to you to learn how to speak English properly and make whatever use you please of it (although the government provides certain subsidies to help you learn to read and write a bit). Otherwise, everybody just sort of pitches in, and somehow the thing evolves on its own, and somehow turns out workable. And interesting. Fascinating, even. . . . "English" as an institution is public property, a public good. Much the same goes for the Internet. Would English be improved if "The English Language, Inc." had a board of directors and a chief executive officer, or a President and a Congress? There'd probably be a lot fewer new words in English, and a lot fewer new ideas. People on the Internet feel much the same way about their own institution. It's an institution that resists

Supercharged Computers

The fastest, most advanced, and most powerful computers in the world are called supercomputers. They are designed to solve highly complex problems that require vast amounts of computer time, such as calculating the behavior of individual molecules in a tornado, or forecasting detailed weather patterns. Most supercomputers being developed today use the principle of parallel computing, which means clusters of computer processors are connected together to create an unbelievably powerful system.

The first supercomputer was developed in the 1970s by a man named Seymour Cray, who introduced the Cray 1. He founded a corporation called Cray Inc., which is now one of the world's leading supercomputer developers. IBM, another top manufacturer, built two systems for the U.S. Department of Energy that are more powerful than all other supercomputers combined. One is called ASCI Purple and is used to simulate aging and the operation of nuclear weapons. The second is known as Blue Gene, and its function is to simulate highly complex physical phenomena, such as weather turbulence or the behavior of high explosives. These supercomputers, which together cost nearly $300 million, are amazingly powerful and fast. Their combined peak speed is as much as 467 trillion calculations per second, a measurement known as teraflops. Blue Gene alone has the capability to process data at a rate of one terabit per second, which is roughly the same as all the data transmitted by ten thousand weather satellites.

IBM claims that its Blue Gene supercomputer is the fastest, most powerful computer in the world.

institutionalization. The Internet belongs to everyone and no one.[24]

Yet even though the Internet does not "belong" to anyone, that does not mean it is not monitored or maintained. Since 1992 a group known as the Internet Society (ISOC) has overseen the formation of policies and protocols that define how people use and interact with the Internet. Subgroups of the ISOC include the Internet Engineering Task Force, the Internet Engineering Steering Group, and the Internet Architecture Board, all of which work together to develop and maintain the Internet's evolving infrastructure.

The ISOC is composed of more than 150 organizations from over 180 countries, and its mission (as stated on the ISOC Web site) is to "assure the open development, evolution and use of the Internet for the benefit of all people throughout the world."[25] Among the organization's goals are monitoring the technical infrastructure of the Internet, including its growth and evolution, and providing forums for the discussion of issues that affect Internet evolution, development, and use. Another goal is to provide current and reliable information about the Internet, including historical data and archives.

Each year, the ISOC sponsors many different programs. For instance, it hosts the annual international conference called INET, which addresses global Internet-related issues. The ISOC also monitors legislation that could impose controls on the Internet and lobbies against excessive regulation. One of its primary areas of focus is education. An ISOC training program called the K-12 Educational Networking Workshop is designed for teachers and administrators, and its Internet Network Technology Workshop trains engineers from developing countries on the operation and management of the Internet. After graduating from the program, many participants have been qualified to im-

plement Internet service in their own countries. ISOC also sponsors the ThinkQuest Internet Challenge, a scholarship program for nine- to nineteen-year-old students. Teams of students who participate in ThinkQuest have six months to build a Web site on any topic within one of the official competition categories. They have opportunities to win prizes, and their award-winning sites gain international exposure.

An exhibitor at a 2005 Internet security conference in Singapore connects to the Internet via a small satellite system.

Could the Infrastructure Collapse?

The Internet Society does a lot to ensure that the Internet continues to thrive—but even the ISOC cannot ensure its longevity. Some experts believe it has grown too fast and expanded too much, and they fear this will lead to its collapse. They also say that terrorism poses a grave risk because if an attack or disaster destroyed one or more major hubs, the Internet itself could begin to come apart. A November 2002 article in *BBC News* was entitled "Risk of Internet Collapse Rising," and another headline in the September 2004 issue of *World Trade Press* warned, "'Beware of the End of the World (Wide Web),' says Intel."

Many computer scientists say the notion of the Internet collapsing is nothing short of nonsense. The Internet was intentionally designed with no central command point or "headquarters"—and that, they insist, guarantees that even if entire networks are destroyed, the infrastructure will still survive. An article entitled "The Internet's Collapse and Other Rumors" states, "There's a notion out there that the threat of cyber-terrorism is somehow threatening the Internet itself. If you follow the mainstream media, you are regularly told about threats that make the Web sound like it's a fragile flower, clinging to dear life. . . . It would help if more people focused on the facts, instead of theories."[26] Author Gus Venditto, who is the editor in chief of the internet.com and EarthWeb.com networks, insists the Internet is a resilient system that was built to be self-healing. So even if it bends, there is no possible way it can break.

To study the potential risk for the Internet's collapse, a team of scientists from Ohio State University conducted an extensive research project that involved simulations of attacks on key Internet hubs. Because these hubs have become such a vital part of the Internet's ability to function, the researchers determined that the Internet is indeed vulnerable to attack. Geography professor Morton O'Kelly, one of the researchers involved in the study, explains: "If you destroyed a major Internet hub, you would also destroy all the links that are connected to it [which] would have ripple effects throughout the Internet."[27]

Are the Internet's days numbered? Has it become too vulnerable through its growth? Could its infrastructure eventually collapse? It seems there are as many opinions about this as there are packets of data whizzing along its networks. Yet in spite of the disagreement over the Internet's fate, one thing is certain: People all over the world use it every single day—and they expect it to be there wherever and whenever they need it.

Chapter 4

A Million and One Uses

Throughout history, technology has made a perceptible difference in people's lives. The telephone gave them a way to communicate with someone far away by talking, rather than writing letters. The phonograph allowed them to buy records and play their favorite music. Radio brought the world of news, music, and entertainment right into their living rooms, and television combined the sounds of radio with moving pictures on a screen. All these technological inventions improved and enhanced people's lives—yet none of them has even come close to transforming society as much as the Internet has.

A World of Choices

What started as a small network that transferred information from one computer to another has evolved into a worldwide system that people depend on every day of their lives. Research shows that more than 68 percent of Americans regularly use the Internet, with high percentages of users in other countries such as Korea, Japan, Sweden, and Great Britain, among others. These numbers have grown exponentially since the World Wide Web was introduced, and they continue to climb on a monthly, daily, and even hourly basis.

One of the reasons more and more people are using the Internet is because of its ever-expanding capabilities. It provides innumerable ways of communicating, learning, shopping, playing, and working. The Internet offers entertainment and music as well as the ability to purchase a car, invest in the stock market, read magazines and newspapers, book an airline ticket, or make payments from a bank account. It offers people so many different choices, in fact, that many say they could not imagine a life without it.

Mary Raines is one person who fits that description —her way of life would simply not be possible without the Internet. Raines is a New Zealand native who now lives in Japan where she teaches English as a foreign language (EFL), and she relies on the Internet to do her job. She frequently visits Web sites that have been created by other EFL teachers who are willing to share their ideas and instructional meth-

The Internet offers almost unlimited possibilities for use. Here, San Francisco 49er Jerome Davis uses the Internet to study profiles of the opposing team before a game.

ods with teachers from all over the world. Raines says if she is feeling uninspired or comes across a teaching challenge she has not dealt with before, she can find the answers she needs almost immediately. She also finds solutions to other types of problems, as she explains: "Sometimes students ask me questions I can't answer—like maybe cultures and customs of other English-speaking countries besides New Zealand. I can find out about these things quickly on the Web. One reason this is so valuable is because I don't have access to good English libraries here, so the Web is my library for that sort of thing."[28]

Because she is so far from home, Raines relies on the Internet to keep informed about the latest news from New Zealand. The Internet also made it possible for her to complete her graduate degree because she "attended" college in Australia while living in Japan. She explains:

> Even though I am thousands of miles away, the Web allowed me to complete my degree at the university of my choice. I had almost instant access to my professors, via email and bulletin boards that were set up by the Australian university for this purpose. I could also access the university library databases, and then order whatever articles and books I needed. There were so many benefits that I can't even remember them all—I just know I'm deeply grateful that the Internet exists! I highly doubt that I could have finished with my master's in applied linguistics if I'd had to complete my studies any other way but online.[29]

Communicating Across the Globe

Like many people throughout the world, Raines also depends on the Internet to keep in touch with friends and family. She constantly uses e-mail to communicate with people back home in New Zealand, as well as others who live in Australia, Greece, Malaysia, Thailand, England, France, Turkey, Guam, Hong Kong, and the United States. "The Internet literally opens up the whole world to me," she says. "I can correspond with friends who I rarely see, no matter where they live. Many of them are people I've met here in Japan and who moved away, and I would likely have lost touch with them without the Internet. Recently I got in touch with a good friend I met here ten years ago, who had gone off traveling. It was so cool that we found each other— and it was because of the Internet that we did."[30]

Another way people communicate via the Internet is by online chatting, or instant messaging. This type of communication is especially popular because it is like being a member of a virtual community. Online chat rooms allow a group of people to talk at the same time about common interests, and the messages they type in can be immediately seen by everyone in the "room." One example is called Internet Relay Chat, or IRC, which originally started in Finland. IRC is a multi-user chat system where people meet on "channels" (or virtual chat rooms) to talk with each other. Instant messaging, which was originally created by America Online, is a similar idea, but it only allows communication between two people. This feature allows individual users to maintain a list of people they designate as their contacts and to see when any of those people are online. A person who sends an instant message causes a small window to pop up on a "buddy's" screen, making it possible for them to chat back and forth in real time. America Online's Instant Messenger, Yahoo Messenger, and MSN Messenger are all examples of instant messaging programs. One of the most popular is ICQ (an acronym for the phrase "I seek you").

Newsgroups are another type of virtual community, although they are online discussions rather

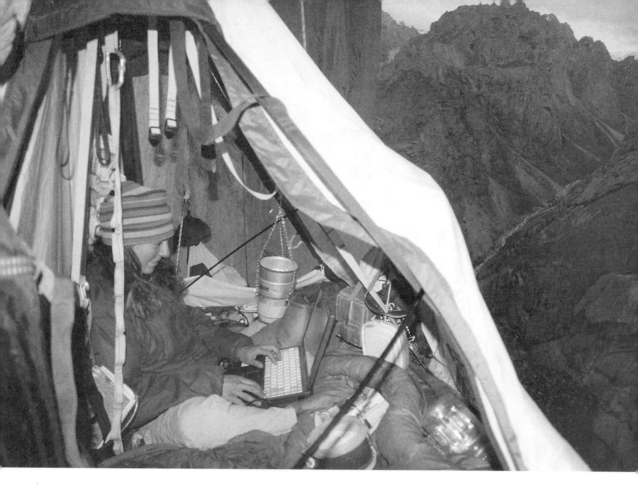

than instant communication. Nancy Ahern participates in a number of newsgroups, and she shares her reasons why:

> We all seek entertainment and companionship. Something good about newsgroups is that they can provide both. Being a software geek does not mean I limit my interests to technical things during the 9 to 5 grind. . . . My interests span topics such as writing, music, history, pets, books, politics, and food. I find newsgroups where like-minded participants are lively, intelligent, and experts in a variety of fields, so that I can learn from them and interact with them. The best part is that I can do this on my time. See, real-life conversations (often called "meatspace" as opposed to "cyberspace") require a

Even while camping in the remote mountains of Pakistan, this woman is able to stay in touch with friends and family via the Internet.

dedicated investment of a chunk of time. Usenet discussions can span days, and you never lose track.[31]

An Information-Rich Resource

In addition to participating in newsgroups, sending e-mails, and chatting with acquaintances online, people also rely on the Internet for the wealth of information they can access. Many depend on it as their primary source of news, and they frequent Web news sites such as *MSNBC News*, *CNN.com*, and *BBC News Online*. Internet news is kept current through constant updating, so sites such as these are espe-

E-mail Hoaxes

The letters often start out with words that immediately grab the reader's attention: "I don't usually send things like this, but I wanted to alert you about something that REALLY HAPPENED to my husband's father's sister's second cousin's attorney's wife and it is very, very scary." People read these e-mails, and many forward them to people they know in an effort to warn others about the "emergency situation." The problem is, such messages are almost always completely false.

Internet hoaxes include fallacies, misinformation, rumors, and common gossip. Some people start them in an attempt to be funny, but readers are often seduced by the apparent seriousness and they pass the messages on. One example is the story of a traveler who awoke in a bathtub full of ice water, only to realize that someone had drugged him and stolen one of his kidneys. The story was a lie. Another was a heartfelt plea for people to help find a nine-year-old girl named Penny Brown who was missing—yet she was reported "missing" in Texas, Australia, Singapore, and Namibia. The rumor was started by an anonymous prankster and the girl never existed in the first place.

One of the best-known hoaxes involves Microsoft founder Bill Gates, and it is still making its way around the Internet. It is presented as a personal message from Gates, promising to pay a thousand dollars to every person who helps him test his new "e-mail tracking software" by forwarding the e-mail to everyone they know. In the hope of receiving a thousand-dollar check, people pass the message on with the statement, "Hey, what do you have to lose?" However, the e-mail is completely without merit because no such promise was ever made.

cially popular with people who want the most up-to-the-minute information.

When people need to do research or seek reference materials of any kind, they need look no further than the Internet. In fact, it is often called the world's biggest library because of the magnitude of materials that are available. The complete text of thousands of periodicals such as newspapers, magazines, and professional journals is online, and many of them can be viewed for free. Others, such as *National Geographic* and the *Wall Street Journal*, are available by subscription or at a fixed fee per article. Also, hundreds of public libraries have their own Web sites that allow visitors to search for books by subject, author, or title, and many allow anyone with a library card to access their online databases. One example is Michigan's eLibrary, which is the virtual home of the Library of Michigan. By entering a valid Michigan driver's license number into a special field on the eLibrary Web site, visitors can access health and science journals, a special genealogy section, librarian's resources, databases specially designed for children and young adults, a number of newspapers, and a wide assortment of periodical databases.

There are also Web sites that provide complete online books. The oldest, which is also one of the largest, is called Project Gutenberg. By visiting the site, visitors can download the complete text of more than thirteen thousand books. Another online book source is Bartleby.com, which was chosen in 2002 by *Yahoo! Internet Life* magazine as the "Best Literary Resource" for the year. Like Project Gutenberg, Bartleby.com offers literary masterpieces as well as scientific papers, historical memoirs, *Bartlett's Familiar Quotations*, the *Columbia Encyclopedia*, the *World Factbook*, and the complete text of the King James Bible, just to name a few.

The availability of online books is increasing every day, and one reason for that is the search engine

A librarian at the New York Public Library scans a public-domain book to make it available on the Internet for downloading free of charge.

Google. Using highly advanced technology, Google is establishing "online reading rooms" for five of the country's major libraries: the University of Michigan, the New York Public Library, Harvard and Stanford Universities, and University of Oxford in England. When the massive project is complete (and it will take years) every single book from Michigan and Stanford will be available online, as will many from the other three libraries—and that amounts to millions of books and billions of pages. Paul LeClerc, president of the New York Public Library, says this is a significant opportunity to bring materials to the rest of the world. "It could solve an old problem: If people can't get to us, how can we get to them?"[32]

Another way people use the Internet to gain knowledge is by learning to speak and write a foreign language. A Web site sponsored by the British Broadcasting Company (BBC) offers online tutorials in French, Spanish, German, and Italian, as well as Greek, Portuguese, and Welsh. Visitors start by using a language gauge, which is designed to help them determine whether they are beginners, quite fluent in a language, or somewhere in between. The comprehensive language courses use video clips and animation to teach how to order food and drink, buy clothes or presents, ask for directions, or chat with an acquaintance. There are also audio magazines, slideshows, quizzes, and games, as well as fact files that provide cultural information about different countries. As someone begins to master a language, there is a learning log that helps monitor progress, as well as tests and challenges designed to help the person move up to the next level of fluency.

Fun, Games, and Culture

Just as people rely on the Internet for information and knowledge, they also use it for fun and entertainment. For instance, PBS.org offers Cyberchase Games Central, a Web site that features a collection of interactive games. All the games are designed to help young people have fun while they are solving math problems and polishing their thinking skills. Another site that combines learning with playing is PrimaryGames.com, which features such interactive games as Bug on a Wire, BADABOOM, Alphabet Zoo, Carve-a-Pumpkin, Adventure Elf, Build-a-Snowman, and Butterfly Match Game, as well as many others. PuzzleFactory.com offers a variety of jigsaw puzzles, memory games, word games, and online coloring books, as well as popular arcade games such as Bubble Shooter, Pacman, Pong 2000, and Space Invaders. ColoringPage.com features connect-the-dot puzzles, mazes, and pages to color, and Yahooligans! Games has a collection of online games such as checkers, backgammon, tic tac toe, chess, and bingo, as well as card games and arcade games.

People also turn to the Internet so they can explore the world's museums. For instance, the National Gallery of Art, located in Washington,

Outfitted with a series of sensors, two French girls play an interactive Internet fighting game in which they take on each other and users around the world.

D.C., has more than five thousand pieces of art from its permanent collection online. Site visitors may search the collection by artist or title, take a virtual tour, or watch a slideshow through streaming video. Italy's Institute and Museum of the History of Science is also available online, and acquaints virtual visitors with its facility through online exhibits and interactive activities. The Louvre, a world-famous art museum located in Paris, has nearly four hundred thousand works of art in its permanent collection. As large as the building is, the Louvre only has enough floor space to display a small percentage of its works of art. However, its entire collection is colorfully displayed on the Web site.

Who Needs the Mall?

If people are interested in French food as much as French art, they may want to do a little online shopping. One Web site called Goûts de France (which means "Tastes of France" in English) offers a unique collection of pastas, seasonings, canned main dishes, jams, honey, dried fruits, and chocolate bars, as well as gourmet gift baskets. Visitors can search by region or by category and select from such French culinary specialties as whole black truffles, sausage with garlic, country pâté, rillettes of goose or pork, sardines in oil, snail casserole with mushrooms, or fish and seaweed soup. Goûts de France also sells merchandise such as table linens, glasses, salad bowls, coffee cups, dessert plates, and platters, all of which are made by French artisans and craftsmen. Orders can be placed online, and Goûts de France ships merchandise from its store in Beaune, France, to customers all over the world.

Gourmet foods are just one example of the wide variety of products available for sale on the Internet. There are online clothing stores, gift stores, toy stores, automotive parts stores, and stores that sell kitchen products and cooking accessories. Shoppers can use the Internet to buy computers, automobiles, motorcycles, sporting goods, furniture, and even pets. Online travel agencies allow people to book Mediterranean cruises, trips to Walt Disney World, ski vacations in the Swiss Alps, or mountain climbing expeditions in Bali.

Online booksellers, such as Amazon.com and Barnes and Noble, are among the most popular sites on the Web. They offer most every book that is available in print and sell millions of titles each year. Raines says that online booksellers are a blessing for her, and she explains why: "In Japan, foreign books [books that are written in English] are expensive, as well as being hard to find. No matter what I need, I can find it on Amazon . . . the only problem is, the selection is so wonderful that I can't visit too often or I'd go broke!"[33] For people interested in purchasing used books, there are numerous links to used booksellers. One online

Traveling the World . . . From Home

Even if people cannot afford to travel around the entire world, they can take a virtual trip on the Internet thanks to Keyhole, Inc., which is based in Mountain View, California. The company has developed an amazingly realistic earth imagery system that uses three-dimensional graphics like those used in videogames. The system combines satellite imagery and aerial photography, and the result is an interactive digital model of Earth. People actually feel as though they are flying through the air and viewing the planet from above as they virtually explore mountains, roads, bike trails, golf courses, and famous world landmarks. Subscribers can type in an address, city, state, or zip code, and then Keyhole zooms in on the location by using the latest NASA satellite maps. A closer look might even reveal a car in the driveway. Then they can take off on their virtual journey, perhaps exploring the Caribbean Islands or visiting the Leaning Tower of Pisa in Italy. On its Web site, Keyhole describes the product as the "ultimate interface to the planet," and entices the would-be traveler by saying: "Fly from space to your home town. Visit exotic locales such as Maui, Tokyo, Rome and Paris. Satellite imagery makes it real. Explore restaurants, hotels, parks and schools. Think magic carpet ride!"

Internet programs using satellite imagery allow users to virtually visit anywhere in the world, including this volcano in Peru.

store that specializes in used books is called A Mystical Unicorn, and its catalog offers more than a hundred thousand different titles. Quigley's Rare Books, whose store is located in the town of Dahlonega, Georgia, offers its collection of rare and hard-to-find books on its Web site, as does Portland, Oregon–based Thaddeus Books.

Shoppers may also purchase common, everyday products on the Internet. For example, the U.S. Postal Service's Web site sells postage stamps for mailing and collecting, and Hallmark.com offers greeting cards and gifts. People who need prescription drugs may purchase them online, and those who want to send flowers can visit virtual florists such as 1800flowers.com. Even groceries can be purchased on the Internet. For instance, shoppers within certain geographic areas who visit Peapod.com can "browse the aisles" at the site and select most every type of grocery item including meats and seafood, fresh produce, baked goods, dairy products, deli items, and even frozen foods such as ice cream. Orders are placed online and then delivered to customers' doors via refrigerated delivery trucks.

One consumer who says she constantly uses the Internet for all kinds of shopping is Randi Trygstad, who lives in West Michigan. Trygstad is an advertising executive as well as the mother of two-year-old twins, and her life is so busy that she has very little time to spare. She shops online for everything from children's clothes to furniture from Pottery Barn, and she explains how valuable that is for her: "The Internet is an amazing timesaver for me, and I simply can't imagine life without it. Last year I did every bit of my Christmas shopping on the Web, and I've also used it to buy gifts for birthdays, weddings, and other occasions. Whenever I need something for Jake and Riley [her twins], I know I'll be able to find it online—even if I can't find it anywhere else."[34]

A German mountain biker shows off his mobile phone equipped with an integrated GPS device that lets him download a bike route from the Internet.

An Incredible Tool

Whether they shop, play games, hear the news, chat with friends, read the Bible, visit the Louvre, or learn to speak Italian, more and more people are turning to the Internet. It opens up the entire world and allows people to live their lives in ways that were not possible in the past. Trygstad shares her thoughts about how the Internet has changed her life: "Ten years ago, if someone had told me I would be so dependent on a computer, I would have looked at them and flatly said they were nuts. But now, when I look at my life and think about all the ways I use the Internet, I don't think I could survive without it. Well I suppose I could . . . somehow. But frankly, I'm spoiled by how much easier it has made life for me."[35]

Chapter 5

The Dark Side

While it is true that the Internet has made life easier, more convenient, and more enjoyable for millions of people, not everything about it is positive. Cybercrime is on the rise, and the story of Amy Boyer is but one example of how dark the Internet can be.

A happy, vivacious twenty-year-old, Amy had many friends, a boyfriend, a job she enjoyed, and her own car. Life was good—but she had no way of knowing that a young man named Liam Youens had long been obsessed with her. He had set up two separate Web sites, and for two years he had freely written about his feelings. On the main page of one of the sites were photos of Amy; an "enter" link led to another page with the headline, "Greetings Infidels, I am Liam Youens," a photo of Youens holding an automatic weapon, and text that read, "Who am I? Well if i had 20 people buried in my backyard my neighbors would have described me as 'Quiet, basically kept to himself.'"[36]

J.A. Hitchcock, one of the nation's leading cybercrime and security experts, says that Youens's obsession with Amy began when they were in the same tenth grade algebra class. He wrote on his Web site that he had been in love with her from that time on, yet she never had any idea, and he posted his thoughts about this, writing: "Oh great, now I'm really depressed, hmmm . . . looks like it's suicide for me. Car accident? Wrists? A few days later I think, 'hey, why don't I kill her, too?'"[37] Hitchcock explains what happened next:

> As he accumulated weapons and ammunition, Liam became braver in his pursuit of Amy. He added a Web page that showed off all the weapons he'd purchased, with descriptions of where he purchased them. . . . Liam wrote on his Web pages about killing Amy's boyfriend and others from the same youth group they belonged to, even a "Columbine-style" shooting at Nashua High School, but Amy remained his primary focus. By the time Liam had worked up his courage to set the date, all it took was less than

Tim and Helen Remsburg pose with a picture of Helen's daughter, Amy, who was killed at work in 1999 by a classmate who used the Internet to find out where she worked.

$100, visits to Web sites where anyone could purchase information, and he had what he needed: the address where Amy worked. He wrote, "It's actually obscene what you can find out about a person on the Internet." On October 15, 1999, at 4:29 P.M., Liam showed up outside the dentist's office where Amy worked part-time. He waited for her to come out and get into her car, and then he drove up alongside her car and shot her several times in the face with his 9mm Glock. He reloaded the gun, put the barrel in his mouth, and killed himself.[38]

Threats on the Web

Hitchcock says that three days before Amy Boyer was killed, she and her mother had been online to do some Web surfing. If they had thought about putting Amy's name into a search engine, they would undoubtedly have found the sites Youens had created—but because they were completely unaware of Youens's obsession, they had no reason to be suspicious or check the Web for her name.

As the tragic Amy Boyer case illustrates, people can be completely unaware that derogatory or threatening material has been posted about them. The Internet has grown so large, with hundreds of millions of people online, that it is a practical impossibility for ISPs or law enforcement agencies to monitor everything that is written online. Even though in their terms of service most ISPs warn subscribers against any sort of harassment, many have no system in place to continuously monitor Web sites and identify threatening information. And in some situations, threats are brought to light but are not taken seriously—even when they are reported to law enforcement personnel.

For example, in the late 1990s Eric Harris, a student at Columbine High School in Colorado, prepared a "hit list" of fellow students he felt had

The Crime of Phreaking

So, let's go back to the year 1972, when I got a phone call from Denny, a blind kid who turned me onto a toy whistle he got out of a Cap'n Crunch cereal box. With this whistle, it was possible to access the internal trunking mechanism of Ma Bell [telephone company]. In conjunction with a blue box (a special tone generating device), it was possible to take internal control of Ma Bell's long distance switching equipment. . . . Naturally, neither the phone companies or the authorities took kindly to my blue box "experiments" I was performing on their equipment, so they tracked me down and filed charges, convicting me under Title 18, Section 1343: Fraud by wire.

Those words were written by John Draper, who is known as the world's most famous "phone phreak." The experiments to which he refers involved a form of cracking known as phreaking—breaking into the telephone network to obtain free long-distance service or to cause other kinds of disruptions. Draper popularized phreaking among the hacking community, and he became known by the hacker handle "Cap'n Crunch." After he was convicted of wire fraud charges in 1976, he spent four months in Lompoc Federal Prison in California. Since then he has held a variety of high-tech positions, and he often gives presentations on computer security issues. He has also created a highly advanced security system for computers known as CrunchBox, which has been called "next to uncrackable."

wronged him somehow, and with whom he planned to get even. He carried a copy of the list in his wallet and posted it on his Web site. Also on the site, Harris and fellow student Dylan Klebold boasted about how they had built pipe bombs from scratch, and they made the declaration, "Now our only problem is to find the place that will be 'ground zero.'"[39] In 1999 Harris and Klebold made good on their threat. Armed with automatic weapons, they went on a shooting spree at their high school, murdering twelve students and injuring dozens, and killing a teacher before taking their own lives. Several years later a shocking piece of evidence surfaced: In 1997 an anonymous tip had alerted sheriff's deputies about Harris's Web site. Although a police report had been filed, the threats were not taken seriously enough to launch a formal investigation. Would such an investigation have prevented the Columbine massacre? No one can say that for sure. But parents of the Columbine victims are convinced their children would likely be alive today if such crucial information had not been swept aside.

The Crime of Cyberstalking

Just as potentially dangerous as threats posted to Web sites is another type of online harassment known as cyberstalking. This can be defined as someone using personal information and communication technology to pursue, track, harass, and/or threaten one or more individuals. Hitchcock had a frightening personal experience with cyberstalking in 1996, after she had publicly challenged a bogus literary agency. She says that the next few years were a nightmare for her, as she was repeatedly harassed and threatened online. Yet the abuse did not stop with the Internet. Hitchcock's home telephone and address as well as her place of employment were posted on various Internet sites, and forged messages allegedly written by her were posted to a number of sex-related newsgroups. Because the posts had been sexually suggestive, Hitchcock began receiving telephone calls in response to the "invitations," and she grew more and more fearful as time went by. She explains:

> I became so paranoid at one point that I would get down on the ground and check under my car before going anywhere. If anyone drove too closely behind me or seemed to be following me, I changed directions, changed lanes, or took a different exit—whatever it took to make sure I wasn't being followed. . . . The mental stress of the whole thing got to be too much and I began to see a psychotherapist. . . . If I hadn't gone to

see her, I don't know how I would have coped. I
know I was on the verge of a mental collapse.[40]

Hitchcock was especially distressed by the lack of
support she received from law enforcement. Upon
contacting the local police, she learned that they
were not computer literate and had no idea what a
newsgroup was. They referred her to the police com-
missioner's office, but when Hitchcock called, a rep-
resentative quickly dismissed her, saying, "I don't
know what to tell ya lady."[41] Even the FBI could not
help her. When she called their computer crimes
unit in Baltimore, Maryland, she was informed that
unless she had received a death threat or threat of
physical harm, or had actually been physically as-
saulted, there was not much they could do. They did
agree to send an FBI agent to talk with her—but she
waited nearly a month for the agent to show up.
Feeling frustrated, angry, and completely fed up,
Hitchcock decided to take matters into her own
hands. She became her own "cybersleuth," and with
the support of friends she calls her "Internet Posse,"
she finally accumulated the proof she needed to
build a case against her harassers. In 2001 they were
prosecuted and punished for their crimes, and one
was sent to prison.
Hitchcock says even though cyberstalking cases
are becoming more common, it is still a relatively
new crime that has only materialized as the Internet
population has skyrocketed. She explains:

Just over seven years ago, cases of cybercrime
were rare, and what is now known as cyberstalking wasn't even acknowledged as a crime. No one
knew what to call it then; some called it online
harassment, online abuse, or cyber-harassment.
But we're not talking about two people arguing
or calling each other bad names. These were inci-
dents where it had gone beyond an annoyance

and had become frightening. As more and more cyberstalking cases occurred and victims reached out to law enforcement for help, all they received were either blank stares or were told to turn off their computers. States didn't have laws in place to protect victims and their harassers kept up the harassment, escalating sometimes to real-life stalking situations.[42]

A technology-crime detective displays the computer system used in an international cyberscam. Rising levels of cybercrime have made Internet security a top priority.

Today cyberstalking is recognized as a crime, and nearly all states have laws against it. Many have cybercrime divisions with officers who are specially trained to catch cyberstalkers. However, in spite of the progress that has been made, many law enforcement agencies are not educated about computer-related crimes, nor are they capable of dealing with them.

One Michigan victim, who does not want to be named, received e-mails in the spring of 2004 from someone who figured out her password and used it to access her ISP account. The sender insinuated that he or she had broken into her computer and gained access to her personal files, and then proved it by referencing information contained in her private e-mails. She shares her story:

> There is no way I can describe the combination of fear, helplessness, and frustration I felt through the whole nightmare—especially when I tried to get help from law enforcement. I've heard stories about how the criminal is often protected more than the victim, and I saw that for myself. I received two e-mails, and the second was clearly threatening . . . not only to myself, but also to my family. But when I went to the local police department, an officer gave me a patronizing smile, took a little notebook out of his pocket, and said, "So, you're here because you received an e-mail?" I felt like I was reporting that a flock of sparrows had built a nest in my garage! I was advised to contact the state police, so I called the nearest branch—but when I explained to the officer on the phone what had happened, he said, "Well there's one problem, ma'am . . . no crime has been committed." Shocked, I said, "You're telling me that someone broke into my e-mail account and used it to send me threatening e-mails, and it's not a CRIME?" And he replied, "No ma'am, only in the movies." At that point I just hung up and thought to myself, Why should I bother?[43]

Hackers and Crackers
Breaking into someone's computer for purposes of harassment is not illegal "only in the movies." But as the Michigan victim found out, even law enforcement

personnel may not be aware of that. The actual crime, however, is cracking rather than hacking, and people commonly confuse the two. Technical expert Eric Steven Raymond defines hackers as expert computer programmers and technology "wizards" who delight in solving problems and overcoming limits. He explains how this mentality differs from computer crackers, whose goal is to engage in criminal activity:

> There is another group of people who loudly call themselves hackers, but aren't. These are people . . . who get a kick out of breaking into computers. . . . Real hackers call these people "crackers" and want nothing to do with them. Real hackers mostly think crackers are lazy, irresponsible, and not very bright, and object that being able to break security doesn't make you a hacker any more than being able to hotwire cars makes you an automotive engineer. Unfortunately, many journalists and writers have been fooled into using the word "hacker" to describe crackers; this irritates real hackers no end. The basic difference is this: hackers build things, crackers break them.[44]

Crackers are tech-savvy criminals who figure out ways to break security codes so they can gain access to other computers—and once they do, they are able to commit a number of crimes. Crackers have been known to harass people, destroy or incapacitate computer systems, and steal bank account information, credit card numbers, or social security numbers. Sometimes these criminals crack into business or government Web sites just for the sake of causing serious damage such as spreading computer viruses or causing entire systems to crash.

One particularly famous cracking case involved the largest international bank robbery in history. Beginning in July 1994 a twenty-three-year-old

Hackers at a 2004 Internet security convention in Malaysia compete with each other to see who can be the first to break a complex computer security code.

Russian mathematician named Vladimir Levin began using his computer to access the Citibank network, from which he obtained a list of customer codes and passwords. Over a period of weeks, he logged onto the system multiple times and transferred more than $10 million into accounts he had set up in the United States and several other countries. Citibank noticed the transfers and contacted law enforcement personnel, who tracked Levin down and arrested him at a London airport in March 1995.

Because Citibank is based in New York, Levin was extradited to the United States and tried in the U.S. district court. After negotiating a plea bargain, he was convicted of stealing $3.7 million and sentenced to three years in prison. He was also ordered to pay $240,015 in restitution to Citibank. After the robbery, Citibank implemented the Dynamic Encryption Card, a security system that is more secure than any other system in the world.

Internet Fraud

In spite of tightened security by Citibank and other organizations, criminal activity is still alive and well on the Internet. One of the most serious cybercrimes is known as identity theft, or the stealing of social security numbers or other personal information with the intention of committing a fraudulent act, typically for financial gain. According to a report by the U.S. Department of Justice, identity theft is one of the fastest-growing crimes, with 161,819 reported cases in the United States in 2002—an increase of more than 500 percent since 2000. With enough personal information about someone, a criminal can assume the victim's identity and conduct a number of crimes. For instance, money can be withdrawn from a bank account, or merchandise can be charged to a credit card without the victim's knowledge. Many identity thieves avoid detection by stealing numerous account numbers and charging only a small amount on each one.

Another type of Internet fraud is known as phishing (tech lingo for "electronic fishing"), and like identity theft, it is fast becoming a serious crime. Experts say that phishing attacks targeted 57 million Internet users during 2003, and about 1.8 million of them became victims of the fraud. Phishers send out e-mails designed with logos and graphics identical to those of well-known Internet businesses such as PayPal or eBay, financial institutions, or credit card issuers. The e-mails use some kind of a hook to entice people into furnishing confidential information such as bank account numbers, user names, or passwords. For instance, recipients may be told their accounts are going to be closed unless they update their personal data. When they click on the supplied link, they are taken to Web sites that look official, complete with actual trademarked graphics—but they are operated by scammers. If unsuspecting consumers actually provide the information requested,

Online Auction Blues

Like other types of Internet crime, online auction fraud is on the rise. According to the Federal Trade Commission (FTC), of the thousands of consumer fraud complaints the agency receives each year, those dealing with online auction fraud consistently rank at or near the top of the list. In addition to failure to ship merchandise, other complaints include shipments of products that are not the same quality as advertised and bogus online payment services. In most cases the complaints involve sellers, but buyers have also been guilty of fraud by not paying for merchandise after they received it.

Another type of fraud is known as "shill" bidding, which is when sellers try to artificially inflate prices by bidding on their own merchandise. One high-profile case on the well-known auction site eBay involved a seller named Kenneth Walton, who listed a painting that he said was done by a famous artist. Its price shot from twenty-five cents to nearly $136,000, but the listing was suspended by eBay after it was discovered that Walton had placed a $4,500 bid of his own. Walton was subsequently investigated by the FBI, and he pled guilty to Internet fraud.

To help combat online auction fraud, eBay goes to great lengths to protect its buyers and sellers. On its Web site there are extensive guidelines and tips, step-by-step tutorials for new customers, and a Security Resolution Center that can be used to report problems. The site also has a feedback feature that allows people to rate each other online. Before buying or selling any merchandise, eBay encourages people to read all feedback that has been posted.

Online auction giant eBay goes to great lengths to protect both buyers and sellers from fraud.

the criminals often use the data for fraudulent acts such as ordering goods and services, making bank transfers, and/or obtaining credit in the name of the consumer.

Can Cybercrime Be Stopped?

From phishing to cracking, from identity theft to cyberstalking, Internet-related crime is definitely on the rise—and as Internet use continues to grow, the situation is expected to get worse. An added complication is that many police departments still lack adequate training in this type of crime, but that is starting to change. For instance, New York City's police force has a computer investigation and technology unit, and many officers have been trained in how to handle computer-related crimes against children. In

Ohio police officers pose as teenage girls in an Internet chat room as part of a sting operation to target sexual predators.

the Chicago suburb of Naperville, Illinois, the police department was one of the first in the nation to launch a high-tech crime investigative unit. In addition, several detectives from the police department are members of the High-Technology Crime Investigation Association, the top organization for computer-crime investigation standards.

Elsewhere, similar efforts are being made to educate and train law enforcement personnel, as well as entire communities, about Internet-related crime. In San Diego, California, the Internet Crimes Against Children Task Force has contributed to numerous arrests and convictions of people who have used the Internet to lure victims and commit crimes. In Dallas, Texas, Operation Avalanche is a program launched by local, state, and federal law enforcement to protect children who use the Internet. In Sioux Falls, South Dakota, the Internet Crimes Against Children Task Force provides public education about online safety and investigates Internet-based crimes against children. And in Seattle, Washington, the police department's special investigations unit has educated hundreds of community members through PTA meetings, special interest group meetings, and the Seattle public schools.

According to Hitchcock, law enforcement agencies throughout the country are encouraging their officers to learn all they can about the Internet and cyber-crime, as well as to work closely with online victim groups such as Working to Halt Online Abuse (WHOA), SafetyEd, and Cyberangels. Many law enforcement personnel are turning to cybercrime experts such as Hitchcock to train officers in tracking down cyberstalkers and dealing with victims. "Cybercrimes are finally getting noticed—and not only by law enforcement, but by the media as well," she says. "This may not exactly be the attention victims want, but at least the word is finally getting out there . . . and law enforcement is listening and learning."[45]

Chapter 6

A Changing World

In an October 2004 interview, ARPANET pioneer Leonard Kleinrock was asked what he believed the next thirty-five years held for the Internet, and he quipped: "Anyone who tries to predict five years out is a fool. So let me try."[46] Kleinrock mused about his involvement in the first network test back in 1969. At that time, he knew the Internet had tremendous potential but even he had no idea how great that potential actually was. In a news release that came out several months before the historic test, Kleinrock predicted that eventually the worldwide network would be everywhere, always on, available all the time, and accessible by people from any location at any time, and invisible just like electricity. He comments about his vision of more than thirty-five years ago: "And, in fact, part of that vision has come about. But the part that I missed is that my 97-year-old mother will be on the Internet today and she is. What I missed was that this is a technology that would allow people to communicate and groups to form. It was not about computers communicating . . . this was a people thing, not a machine thing."[47]

Virtual Communities

Kleinrock's reference to groups is apt because more than any other medium, the Internet has allowed people from all over the world to interact with each other. Paula Light, a writer from Huntington Beach, California, says she has many friends she knows only through the Internet. In November 2004 she joined an online writing group called National Novel Writing Month (NaNoWriMo) 2004, which challenged all participants to write a fifty-thousand word novel in a month. As the time went by they monitored each other's progress, kept up an ongoing chat, and encouraged each other not to give up. Light says the Internet made such an aggressive project possible:

Patrons of a cybercafé in Paris surf the Internet. The Internet allows people all over the world to interact with each other in real time.

> I accepted the challenge—and then almost immediately wondered if I'd taken on more than I could handle. It was a monstrous amount of work to accomplish in just one month, and I'm

Members of a design team at Daimler Chrysler use virtual-reality headsets and other equipment to collaborate on a new car design.

convinced that being connected to this virtual community of friends is what kept me going. We simply would not let each other fail. We shared the same passion about writing, as well as the drive to cross the finish line before November 30th. Amazingly enough, I succeeded in meeting my goal of fifty thousand words, and many of my fellow writers did as well. I've never met any of them face to face, yet because of this experience, I feel as though I've known them for years.[48]

The Internet's "virtual community" aspect is expected to grow increasingly important as technology becomes more sophisticated. Experts say that in the future, people will sit at their computers and feel as though they are in the same room with friends who are halfway across the globe. This will be possible because of virtual reality, which is a collection of digital and graphic techniques that are used to build computer-generated "worlds." Virtual reality seems so real that it has been called "surround sound for the mind." According to Michael Donfrancesco, an executive with a company called InterSense that makes virtual reality equipment, it will not be long before people do much more than just surf the Internet—they will be immersed inside it. Internet users of the future may wear personal headsets that allow them to interact with the Web in three dimensions by "walking through" scenes that are now visible only on two-dimension computer monitors. Future technology will likely be even more advanced, making headsets obsolete.

The Web site Living Internet explains how virtual reality technology will work with the Internet of the future:

> There will come a day when you will be able to have dinner with a group of friends each in a different city, almost as though you were in the same room, although you will all have to bring your own food. Virtual reality applications will not only better and better reflect the natural world, they will also have the fluidity, flexibility, and speed of the digital world, layered on the Internet, and so will be used to create apparently magical environments of types we can only now begin to imagine. These increasingly sophisticated virtual experiences will continue to change how we understand the nature of reality, experience, art, and human relations.[49]

"Smart Homes"

Not only will the future Internet continue changing the way people interact with each other; it will also transform how they live inside their own homes. Tomorrow's appliances are being designed with built-in intelligence—in other words, they are programmed to do their own thinking. Homes of the future are referred to as "smart homes," because it is likely they will be equipped with a variety of intelligent, Internet-ready appliances.

One example of such a futuristic appliance is a washing machine called the Margherita 2000, which was developed by an Italian manufacturer called Merloni. The machine has an internal computer complete with a cellular phone that allows it to connect to the Internet. It is programmed to scan the washing instructions of clothes and then consult the Internet to find out the right soap to use and the correct temperature for the water. If the machine detects that the temperature is too high or the detergent has been incorrectly measured, it will send out warning codes to the manufacturer. In addition, it is designed to sense when it needs updates. If new software is needed for the washing machine to run properly, it can simply download its own upgrades from the Internet.

Another unique appliance is an Internet-linked microwave oven. Introduced by Sharp Electronics Corporation in Japan, the microwave allows consumers to download recipes from the company's Web site, which it then stores in its memory. When a meal is ready to cook, the microwave can retrieve necessary information about cooking times, power levels, temperatures, and cooking sequence, so the recipe is perfectly prepared.

The refrigerators of tomorrow will also be Internet savvy. Experts predict that these smart appliances will be equipped with internal computers and touch screens on the door, as well as built-in microphones and cameras so family members can leave video or e-mail messages for each other. This type of refrigerator, which is already in development by several manufacturers, will have a built-in device that allows it to connect to the Internet. If the appliance detects that milk is sour or vegetables are spoiled, it can add these items to a digital shopping list and then beam the list directly to an online grocer such as Peapod. Then, depending on what the consumer has programmed in, the groceries could either be delivered or picked up at the store.

The smart home of tomorrow will also be of great benefit to senior citizens because it will allow them to live more independently. One example is Home Assurance, a system developed by General Electric (GE) that can provide added security to seniors who have health problems or any kind of special needs. The system features a network of wireless motion detectors that can be installed in various locations throughout someone's home. Sensors will monitor

To ensure foolproof operation, household appliances of the future, like this futuristic rice cooker, will interface with the Internet.

the person's activity and continuously transmit the data over the Internet to a server at GE. Caregivers or family members can log into the GE server whenever they want to check up on someone, or they can program the device to update them automatically by telephone or e-mail.

Security and Privacy

Just as technology in a home could provide peace of mind for family members who are concerned about their aging relatives, future software could also provide computer users with added security. For example, Microsoft is developing software they say is a tool that will help consumers keep crackers out, guard against harmful viruses, and even block spam mail. Known as the Next-Generation Secure Computing Base (formerly called Palladium), the software is designed to make computers more secure, with built-in security and privacy functions. The idea is to create a virtual vault inside the Windows operating system, in which users could create their own "safe deposit boxes" for storing encrypted data. The information would then be accessible only to those software programs, people, and Web sites that the computer recognizes as being authorized to see it. For instance, if someone tried to forward an e-mail that was intended for one recipient only, the software would ensure that anyone else received only gibberish. Users who forgot to pay the bill for an online music subscription would be unable to decrypt the tunes they had downloaded until the payment was received.

Not everyone believes this sort of technology is positive—in fact, some people are adamantly opposed to it. They argue that the real purpose of such software is to control users by influencing how they interact with the Internet. Richard Stallman, founder of the Free Software Foundation, calls this technology "treacherous computing," and he explains his

The Universe Wide Web?

The Internet allows people to talk to each other instantly, no matter where they are located in the world. Now, scientists are exploring instant communication *beyond* this planet, and they say that the future Internet will expand far into the solar system. This would give astronauts who visit Mars and other distant planets the ability to communicate instantaneously with scientists back on Earth—even though they will be separated by hundreds of millions of miles. This is a crucial part of the space exploration program because current methods of communication are extremely slow. For instance, during the 1997 Mars *Pathfinder* mission, data from the spacecraft trickled back to Earth about two hundred times slower than data is currently transferred on the Internet.

A team of scientists, engineers, and programmers are working together to develop an interplanetary Internet, which will be made up of three basic components. The first is NASA's Deep Space Network (DSN), an international network of antennas that is the largest and most sensitive scientific telecommunications system in the world. The other two components include a six-satellite constellation around Mars and a new protocol for transferring data.

There are many challenges that must be overcome before the interplanetary Internet becomes a reality, and one of the largest is security. Crackers pose the worst threat to the system, because deliberate damage to navigation or communication systems could be disastrous for space missions, as well as life-threatening for astronauts. The developers are taking every precaution to design a system that will be absolutely impenetrable to crackers—something that has never been possible on Earth.

This illustration depicts a satellite that will serve as the hub for a future interplanetary Internet system.

reasons for that perception: "Large media corporations, together with computer companies such as Microsoft and Intel, are planning to make your computer obey them instead of you. Proprietary programs have included malicious features before, but this plan would make it universal."[50]

A different (although related) issue that has many people concerned is one of the continued erosion of consumers' privacy. The Internet was designed as a completely open medium, and its creators are still convinced that it should remain that way—yet there are disadvantages to the free-flowing distribution of information. According to the Web site Privacy and Spying.com, many of the features expected of the future Internet will inevitably lead to a serious invasion of privacy. The site warns:

> As more and more of the products we use each day become Internet-connected, the personal information they collect will be fed to marketers —and bought and sold without our knowledge or consent. Those eggs your fridge has been ordering online for you—coupled with some high-fat foods and cheeses—set off a few warning bells at your insurance company which recently purchased this information. Don't be surprised to see your premiums go up next year, or when ads for cholesterol-lowering products start to appear on your PC. . . . As digital television emerges, our viewing habits will also be tracked by companies who monitor what we watch, when we watch it and what we buy. Spending a lot of time on the home-shopping channel? Be prepared for a slew of invasive marketing aimed at you for varied products and services. Tuned in to the Playboy Channel last night? Watch out for adult advertisements next time your daughter logs onto the Net from the home computer.[51]

Whether or not this alarming prediction is accurate is uncertain. Kleinrock agrees that the Internet has added to consumers' loss of privacy, but he says it is something that cannot be helped. His perspective is that if people want to avail themselves of the Internet's advantages, they must be able to cope with the loss of privacy that goes along with it. "I think it's a lost cause right now. You can't put that genie back in the box. Just like you can't put spam back in the box. It's out there and you have to learn to live with it . . . [but] hang in there . . . the important thing is to find ways to use this technology to enhance the things you do."[52]

Advertising Trends

It is not only consumers who use the Internet to enhance the things they do; businesses are also flocking to the Web to advertise their products and services. In fact, the Internet is transforming marketing and advertising—a $1 trillion industry—and has given advertisers access to millions of people all over the world. Also, Internet advertising is more targeted and can be more closely tracked than traditional media such as television, radio, and billboards. One advertising method that is offered by Google is called AdWords. When someone uses the search engine and types in keywords, specially targeted links automatically pop up that can take the person to an advertiser's site.

For instance, if a person wants to make homemade sourdough bread and types the words "sourdough starter" into the Google search field, this nets an overwhelming number of choices—nearly sixty thousand links. However, on the right side of the screen links are displayed that advertisers have paid for, one of which is www.sourdoughbreads.com. The owner of the site, Linda Wilbourne, says she is sold on advertising with AdWords because it is so affordable compared to other types of advertising. She did not have to sign any contracts and, along with a minimal monthly fee, she only has to pay if someone clicks on her link. Many companies share Wilbourne's enthusiasm for this type of "pay-per-click" advertising, which *Economist* magazine equates with paying for the delivery of junk mail only to households that read it.

Not all Internet advertising is inexpensive, though. According to *Business Week Online*, companies that want ads to appear on heavily trafficked sites such as America Online, Yahoo!, and Microsoft Network must pay astronomical amounts of money —as much as three hundred thousand dollars for just twenty-four hours on a home page. But because the Internet population is growing so fast, savvy advertisers know that it is an excellent way to reach consumers and they are more than willing to pay the price. For instance, in 2003 Ford Motor Company used the Internet to unveil its new F-150 pickup truck. On the day of the launch Ford placed bold banner ads on three major Web sites for twenty-four hours. Based on the number of regular visitors to the sites, Ford estimated that about 50 million Web surfers would see the ads, and they were right. Millions of people clicked into them, which caused traffic on Ford's Web site to soar at three thousand clicks per second. This led to a 6 percent increase in sales over the first three months of the advertising campaign, and Ford representatives directly attribute that success to the Internet.

Many companies share Ford's philosophy about online advertising, and it is becoming a regular part of their annual media buys. *Business Week* says that the average growth rate for the entire advertising industry is 7.7 percent per year—while Internet advertising alone is growing at nearly 30 percent per year.

Looking Ahead

With the Internet population continuing to increase at an astounding rate, there will be many

Wireless Web

Internet pioneer Leonard Kleinrock has a futuristic concept about the Internet that he calls "nomadic access." In an October 2004 interview with Rick Boguski on *CBC News Online* he described it:

> Most people believe cyberspace is behind the screen on their computers. What's necessary is that we take it out of that screen and into the physical world, their familiar environment, in the desk, in the walls, on the floor, in your shoes, in your eyeglasses, on your belt and in your automobile. . . . Everywhere you go you should be able to have this nomadic access and these smart spaces, this intelligent environment I'm talking about.

Whether or not the Internet will be quite as ubiquitous as Kleinrock envisions is not certain. However, wireless technology will certainly change the way people access the Internet.

Wireless Internet works by sending radio signals to and from a remote antenna. The most important factor in its development has been the growth of digital cellular phones, which use wireless technology to connect to the Internet. In 1997 Nokia, Motorola, Ericsson, and Phone.com joined together to create a special protocol called the Wireless Application Protocol (WAP). In the same way the Internet uses protocols so networks can talk to each other, the WAP will be used to create an Internet that is completely wireless.

At this point, cell phones and personal digital assistants (PDAs) provide access to the Internet from most anywhere. Yet as handy as these devices are, they cannot give users the same level of Internet activity as a regular computer because most Web sites will not work with the WAP. That will change, however, as more and more people demand remote Internet access. Whether they will demand it in their eyeglasses, on their belts, or in their shoes is still one of life's great unknowns.

This wireless, head-mounted device projects a virtual image of the Internet in the operator's field of vision.

challenges in the future. As more and more people hook in, there will be an increased need for technology that is capable of preventing traffic jams, as well as furnishing ample bandwidth to handle an astronomical amount of information. Experts say this need will be met by wireless technology such as satellite links, which will eventually replace wires and cables. This means that in the future the Internet will be able to provide as much, or perhaps even more, mobility as people currently enjoy with cell phones.

One entity that has been instrumental in developing emerging Internet technologies is known as Internet2, which is a partnership between universities, technology companies, and government agencies. Internet2 is a consortium of hundreds of high-speed networks linked together by fiber-optic backbones that span the United States as well as link to other countries. It transmits data at speeds that are faster than the speed of light, and it creates massive increases in bandwidth—and as a result, the Internet is becoming more powerful and valuable than it has ever been before. For instance, Internet2 could allow scientists throughout the world to share specialized equipment such as electron microscopes, and doctors could share high-resolution X-ray images in real time instead of downloading digital photographs. Because of its tremendous potential, Internet2 is being hailed as the Internet of the future.

Although Kleinrock was one of the original Internet pioneers, even he could never have imagined its seemingly infinite possibilities. He is convinced that tomorrow's Internet will have an even greater effect on education, as well as how people work, play, and live their lives. In spite of its dark side, including crime, computer viruses, spam mail, and the loss of privacy, Kleinrock hopes people will believe that its advantages far outweigh the problems. He shares his thoughts:

I think it's the most magnificent distribution mechanism I've ever seen. And the thing that gives it this power is that it allows many people to interact in an open culture, open research, shared applications, shared ideas. That culture and basically that community of people, that combination, is what gives it its power and that's what we have to preserve at the very high level as we move ahead into the future.[53]

Notes

Introduction: The World on a Desktop

1. Jennifer Rasmussen, interview by author, August 1, 2004.
2. U.S. Department of Commerce, "The Emerging Digital Economy," April 1998. www.technology.gov/digeconomy/emerging.htm.

Chapter 1: The Roots of the Internet

3. Paul Raeburn, *Uncovering the Secrets of the Red Planet*. Washington, DC: National Geographic Society, 1998, p. 47.
4. Joseph C.R. Licklider, "Man-Computer Symbiosis," March 1960, in *In Memoriam: J.C.R. Licklider*, Digital Systems Research Center, August 7, 1990. http://memex.org/licklider.pdf.
5. Bruce Sterling, "Short History of the Internet," *Magazine of Fantasy and Science Fiction*, February 1993. www.library.yale.edu/div/instruct/internet/history.htm.
6. Sterling, "Short History of the Internet."
7. Massachusetts Institute of Technology, "Vinton Cerf: Internet Protocols (TCP/IP)," July 2000. http://web.mit.edu/invent/iow/cerf.html.
8. Sterling, "Short History of the Internet."

Chapter 2: Enter the World Wide Web

9. Tim Berners-Lee, *Weaving the Web: The Original Design and Ultimate Destiny of the World Wide Web by Its Inventor*. New York: HarperCollins, 1999, pp. 4–5.
10. *Enquire Within upon Everything*. London: Houlston and Sons, 1884, title page. www.gutenberg.org/dirs/1/0/7/6/10766/10766-h/10766-h.htm.
11. Berners-Lee, *Weaving the Web*, p. 15.
12. Berners-Lee, *Weaving the Web*, p. 16.
13. Berners-Lee, *Weaving the Web*, p. 27.

14. Tim Berners-Lee, "Frequently Asked Questions," World Wide Web Consortium. www.w3.org/People/Berners-Lee/FAQ.html#What2.
15. Berners-Lee, *Weaving the Web*, p. 36.
16. Tim Berners-Lee, "WorldWideWeb—Executive Summary," alt.hypertext newsgroup, August 6, 1991. http://groups.google.com/groups?selm=6487%40cernvax.cern.ch.
17. Quoted in Paul Festa, "Turning On the World Wide Web," *News.com*, December 10, 2001. http://news.com.com/2008-1082-276771.html?legacy=cnet.
18. Berners-Lee, *Weaving the Web*, p. 209.

Chapter 3: How the Internet Works

19. Peter Kent, *The Complete Idiot's Guide to the Internet*. Indianapolis, IN: Que, 1994, p. 14.
20. Nancy Ahern, interview by author, November 15, 2004.
21. Find an ISP, "ISP Checklist." www.findanisp.com/choose.php.
22. Sterling, "Short History of the Internet."
23. HowStuffWorks, "How Internet Infrastructure Works." http://computer.howstuffworks.com/internet-infrastructure.htm.
24. Sterling, "Short History of the Internet."
25. Internet Society, "Internet Society Mission Statement." www.isoc.org/isoc/mission.
26. Gus Venditto, "The Internet's Collapse and Other Rumors," *InternetNews.com*, January 31, 2003. www.internetnews.com/commentary/article.php/1577541.
27. Quoted in *BBC News*, "Risk of Internet Collapse Rising," November 26, 2002. http://news.bbc.co.uk/2/hi/technology/2514651.stm.

Chapter 4: A Million and One Uses

28. Mary Raines, interview by author, November 1, 2004.

29. Raines, interview.
30. Raines, interview.
31. Ahern, interview.
32. Quoted in Michael Liedtke, "U-M's Entire Library to Appear on Google," *Muskegon Chronicle*, December 14, 2004, pp. 1A, 4A.
33. Raines, interview.
34. Randi Trygstad, interview by author, September 16, 2004.
35. Trygstad, interview.

Chapter 5: The Dark Side

36. Quoted in AmyBoyer.org. www.amyboyer.org/mind.htm.
37. Quoted in J.A. Hitchcock, *Net Crimes & Misdemeanors: Outmaneuvering the Spammers, Swindlers, and Stalkers Who Are Targeting You Online*. Medford, NJ: Information Today, 2003, p. 112.
38. Hitchcock, *Net Crimes & Misdemeanors*, pp. 112–14.
39. Quoted in *CBSNews.com*, "Did Cops Miss Columbine Tip?" October 30, 2003. www.cbs news.com/stories/2004/02/26/national/main602339.s html.
40. Hitchcock, *Net Crimes & Misdemeanors*, p. 14.
41. Quoted in Hitchcock, *Net Crimes & Misdemeanors*, pp. 14–15.
42. J.A. Hitchcock, interview by author, November 20, 2004.
43. Anonymous, interview by author, November 1, 2004.
44. Eric Steven Raymond, "How to Become a Hacker," Thyrsus Enterprises, 2001. www.catb.org/~esr/faqs/hacker-howto.html.
45. Hitchcock, interview.

Chapter 6: A Changing World

46. Quoted in Rick Boguski, "The Past and Future of

the Internet," *CBC News Online*, October 29, 2004. www.cbc.ca/news/background/internet/kleinrock_interview.html.

47. Quoted in Boguski, "The Past and Future of the Internet."

48. Paula Light, interview by author, December 1, 2004.

49. Bill Stewart, "The Future of the Internet," *Living Internet*. http://livinginternet.com/i/ia_future.htm.

50. Quoted in Robert Lemos, "Trust or Treachery: Security Technologies Could Backfire Against Consumers," *CNET News.com*, November 7, 2002. http://news.com.com/Trust+or+treachery/2009-1001_3-964628.html.

51. Privacy and Spying.com, "Internet Privacy Today." www.privacyandspying.com/privacy-future.html.

52. Quoted in Boguski, "The Past and Future of the Internet."

53. Quoted in Boguski, "The Past and Future of the Internet."

Glossary

ARPANET: A project of the Advanced Research Projects Agency (ARPA), this was the name of the original network that evolved into the Internet.

backbone: A high-speed interconnecting network composed of fiber-optic trunk lines, satellite links, and powerful computing and switching equipment.

bandwidth: The amount of information an Internet service provider (ISP) can transmit at any given time.

browser: A program that opens and displays Internet documents on a user's computer monitor.

cracker: Someone who accesses computers illegally with the intention of committing a crime; often confused with hackers, whose intention is not to commit criminal acts.

domain name system (DNS): A code that denotes the type of organization (such as .com or .org) that owns a particular Web site.

host: A computer on a network that provides services to other computers.

hypertext: A unique system that enables links (known as hyperlinks) to connect documents and programs on one computer as well as between separate computers.

hypertext markup language (HTML): A format that allows links to remain hidden within Web pages and provides access to other places within a Web site and to other sites on the Internet.

hypertext transfer protocol (HTTP): A programming language that allows Web pages to be linked together on computers across the Internet.

Internet Society: A group that oversees the formation of policies and protocols that define how people use and interact with the Internet.

intranet: A privately owned internal network most often used for communication and exchange of information within a company.

local area network (LAN): A network of computers that are connected either through wires and cables or through wireless connections.

network access point (NAP): Network exchange facilities that serve as the hubs of the Internet.

phishing: The crime of using legitimate-looking e-mails or Web sites to trick people into revealing personal information such as account numbers and passwords.

protocols: A set of rules and instructions that computers use to talk to one another.

routers: Specialized behind-the-scenes computers that bridge networks together and are controlled by internal configuration tables.

uniform resource locator (URL): Originally called the universal resource identifier, this is a method of assigning Web sites their own unique addresses on the Internet.

Usenet: A worldwide system of discussion groups called newsgroups.

Web server: A program that allows Web documents stored on one computer to be accessed by other computers.

World Wide Web: The worldwide information space that connects billions of hypertext documents located throughout the Internet.

WorldWideWeb: Tim Berners-Lee's first hypertext software program featuring a point-and-click browser.

For Further Reading

Books

David Jefferis, *Internet: Electronic Global Village*. New York: Crabtree, 2002. Includes a brief history of the Internet's development as well as various aspects of the Web, commerce, communication, and other general information.

Ken Leebow, *1001 Incredible Things for Kids on the Internet*. New York: Warner, 2002. Designed to help young people get the most out of the Internet, this book includes tips for "happy and safe surfing" and information about a variety of Web sites that are educational, entertaining, and/or useful.

Art Wolinsky, *The History of the Internet and the World Wide Web*. Berkeley Heights, NJ: Enslow, 1999. A friendly, easy-to-understand introduction to Internet and Web history, including their history and growth. Also offers students helpful tips on using the Internet for research and homework.

Periodicals

Jeff Howe, "The Shadow Internet," *Wired*, January 2005.

Jennifer Kahn, "The Homeless Hacker v. the New York Times," *Wired*, April 2004.

Monkeyshines, "The Information Age: Computers and the Internet," July 2001.

Kristina Nwazota, "Online Stores May Ease Tension Between Music Industry, Fans," *NewsHour Extra*, May 8, 2003.

Clive Thompson, "The BitTorrent Effect," *Wired*, January 2005.

David L. Wilson, Jon Healey, and Sam Diaz, "Hackers Cripple Web Sites," *San Jose Mercury News*, February 9, 2000.

Web Sites

HowStuffWorks (www.howstuffworks.com). An information-rich site that includes many facts about the Internet's infrastructure as well as Web servers, routers, cable modems, and more.

Internet 101 (www.internet101.org). An excellent site that covers Internet and Web history and also provides basic information about newsgroups, e-mail, chatting, surfing, and online safety.

The Internet Society (ISOC) (www.isoc.org). Includes general information about the ISOC organization as well as Internet history, articles, and links to other Internet-related Web sites.

Learn the Net (www.learnthenet.com). A "how-to" site for anyone interested in the Internet, visitors can learn about search engines, smart and safe online shopping, and Web publishing, as well as take a "Web-at-a-Glance" tutorial.

Living Internet (http://livinginternet.com). An exceptionally well-organized and comprehensive source for learning about Internet history.

Working to Halt Online Abuse (WHOA) (www.haltabuse.org). The official Web site of WHOA, whose mission is "to educate the Internet community about online harassment, empower victims of harassment, and formulate voluntary policies that systems administrators can adopt in order to create harassment-free environments."

Works Consulted

Books

Tim Berners-Lee, *Weaving the Web: The Original Design and Ultimate Destiny of the World Wide Web by Its Inventor.* New York: HarperCollins, 1999. The fascinating story of how the Web came to be as told by the man responsible for its creation.

J.A. Hitchcock, *Net Crimes & Misdemeanors: Outmaneuvering the Spammers, Swindlers, and Stalkers Who Are Targeting You Online.* Medford, NJ: Information Today, 2003. Written by a nationally known cybercrime expert, this book is both eye-opening and informative about most every kind of Internet crime.

Peter Kent, *The Complete Idiot's Guide to the Internet.* Indianapolis, IN: Que, 1994. An excellent guide to the Internet written in easy-to-understand language. Includes many sidebars with interesting anecdotes and fun facts.

Paul Raeburn, *Uncovering the Secrets of the Red Planet.* Washington, DC: National Geographic Society, 1998. A book about the exploration of the planet Mars.

Periodicals

Michael Liedtke, "U-M's Entire Library to Appear on Google," *Muskegon Chronicle*, December 14, 2004.

Internet Sources

BBC News, "Risk of Internet Collapse Rising," November 26, 2002. http://news.bbc.co.uk/2/hi/technology/2514651.stm.

Tim Berners-Lee, "Frequently Asked Questions," World Wide Web Consortium. www.w3.org/People/Berners-Lee/FAQ.html #What2.

————, "WorldWideWeb—Executive Summary," alt.hypertext newsgroup, August 6, 1991. http://groups.google.com/groups?selm=6487%40cernvax.cern.ch.

Rick Boguski, "The Past and Future of the Internet," *CBC News Online*, October 29, 2004. www.cbc.ca/news/background/internet/kleinrock_interview.html.

CBSNews.com, "Did Cops Miss Columbine Tip?" October 30, 2003. www.cbsnews.com/stories/2004/02/26/national/main602339.shtml.

Enquire Within upon Everything. London: Houlston and Sons, 1884. www.gutenberg.org/dirs/1/0/7/6/10766/10766-h/10766-h.htm.

Paul Festa, "Turning On the World Wide Web," *News.com*, December 10, 2001. http://news.com.com/2008-1082-276771.html?legacy=cnet.

Find an ISP, "ISP Checklist." www.findanisp.com/choose.php.

Susannah Fox, Janna Quitney Anderson, and Lee Rainie, "The Future of the Internet," Pew Internet & American Life Project, January 9, 2005. www.pewinternet.org/pdfs/PIP_Future_of_Internet.pdf.

Craig C. Freudenrich, "How Fiber Optics Work," HowStaffWorks. http://electronics.howstuffworks.com/fiber-optic.htm.

Charles Herzfeld, "Charles Herzfeld on ARPAnet and Computers," *About.com*. http://inventors.about.com/library/inventors/bl_Charles_Herzfeld.htm.

HowStuffWorks, "How Internet Infrastructure Works." http://computer.howstuffworks.com/internet-infrastructure.htm.

Internet Society, "Internet Society Mission Statement." www.isoc.org/isoc/mission.

Robert Lemos, "Trust or Treachery: Security Technologies Could Backfire Against Consumers," *CNET News.com*, November 7, 2002. http://news.com.com/Trust+or+treachery/2009-1001_3-964628.html.

J.C.R. Licklider, "Man-Computer Symbiosis," March 1960, in *In*

Memoriam: J.C.R. Licklider, Digital Systems Research Center, August 7, 1990. http://memex.org/licklider.pdf.

Massachusetts Institute of Technology, "Vinton Cerf: Internet Protocols (TCP/IP)," July 2000. http://web.mit.edu/invent/iow /cerf.html.

Privacy and Spying.com, "Internet Privacy Today." www.privacy andspying.com/privacy-future.html.

Eric Steven Raymond, "How to Become a Hacker," Thyrsus Enterprises, 2001. www.catb.org/~esr/faqs/hacker-howto.html.

Bruce Sterling, "Short History of the Internet," *Magazine of Fantasy and Science Fiction*, February 1993. www.library.yale.edu/div/ instruct/internet/history.htm.

Bill Stewart, "The Future of the Internet," *Living Internet*. http:// livinginternet.com/i/ia_future.htm.

U.S. Department of Commerce, "The Emerging Digital Economy," April 1998. www.technology.gov/digeconomy/emerging.htm.

Gus Venditto, "The Internet's Collapse and Other Rumors," *InternetNews.com*, January 31, 2003. www.internetnews.com/ commentary/article.php/1577541.

Web Sites

AmyBoyer.org (www.amyboyer.org/mind.htm). The site created by Amy Boyer's family and friends to educate others about the type of cybercrime that was responsible for her death.

John T. Draper (http://webcrunchers.com/crunch). The official site of John Draper, known as the world's most famous phone phreak.

Index

addresses, 20–21, 26, 32–33, 47
advertising, 90–92
AdWords, 91–92
alt.hypertext, 34
Amazon.com, 63
America Online, 43, 56, 92
Andreessen, Marc, 36
appliances, 85–87
Archie (search tool), 29
ARPA (Advanced Research Projects Agency), 12–15, 24
ARPANET (ARPA Network), 15–25, 39
articles, 23
ASCI Purple (computer), 49
astronauts, 37, 89
auction fraud, 79

backbones, 23, 40, 44–46, 48, 94
bandwidth, 42–44, 94
banking, 76–77
Barnes and Noble, 63
Bartleby.com, 59
BBC News Online, 58
Bell Laboratories, 19
Bellovin, Steve, 23
Berners-Lee, Tim, 27–34, 38
bill paying, 7, 88
Bina, Eric, 36
Blue Gene (computer), 49
booksellers, 63, 65
  see also e-books
Boyer, Amy, 68–70
browsers, 31–36
bulletin boards, 55
businesses, 7, 40, 44, 94

cables, 9, 33, 40–42, 44, 94
Cailliau, Robert, 31, 34
Cap'n Crunch. See Draper, John
cell phones, 93, 94
Cerf, Vinton, 21–22, 24

CERN, 27–32, 34–35, 38
channels, 56
chat rooms, 7, 56, 58
children, 7
  crimes against, 80–81
Citibank, 77–78
cladding, 42
clients, 29, 32, 41
CNN.com, 58
codes, 25, 47, 76
Cold War, 12–13
ColoringPage.com, 61
Columbine High School, 69, 70–72
commands, 26–27
commercial sites, 25
  see also shopping
communication, 7
  global, 14–15, 21, 55–58, 82–85
  interplanetary, 89
companies, 7, 40, 44, 94
Compuserv, 43–44
computers
  as communication devices, 14–18, 35–36
  linking of, 9, 12, 20–26, 29–32, 40–41
  see also hosts; routers
configuration tables, 47–48
crackers, 71, 75–77, 88, 89
Cray, Seymour, 49
crime, 68–81
CrunchBox, 71
culture, 61–62
Cyberchase Games Central, 61
cybercrime, 68–81
CyberScalpel, 37
cyberspace, 57, 93
cyberstalking, 72–75
cyberterrorism, 51–52

Dallas, Texas, 81

data
   encrypted, 77, 88
   transmission of, 15–17, 21, 26–27,
     40, 46–49, 89, 94
databases, linking of, 30, 35–36, 59
Deep Space Network (DSN), 89
discussion groups, 23–24, 43,
   56–58
distance learning, 54–55
DNS (domain name system), 25
doctors, 37, 94
documents, linking of, 29, 32–34
Draper, John, 71
Dynamic Encryption Card, 77

earth imagery systems, 64
eBay, 79
e-books, 7, 59–60
education, 7, 25, 50–51, 54–55, 61,
   94
1800flowers.com, 65
electricity, 42, 82
electronic fishing, 78
eLibrary, 59
Ellis, Jim, 23
e-mail, 7, 18, 20, 23, 43, 55–58, 75,
   78, 88
energy, light, 42
English, teaching of, 54–55
Enquire, 28–30, 32, 38
entertainment, 7, 61–62
Europe, 45
European Conference on
   Hypertext, 31

FBI (Federal Bureau of
   Investigation), 73, 79
Federal Reserve Board, 18
fiber-optics, 9, 40–42, 44, 94
files, 29, 43
file servers, 41
foods, 63, 65
Ford Motor Company, 92
FORTH-net, 45
fraud, 78–80
future, 82–95

games, 7, 61, 64
GARR-B, 45
Gates, Bill, 58

gateways, 25
GÉANT, 45
geeks, 26, 57
General Electric (GE), 87
geographical locations, 25
Golden Telecom, 45
Google, 60, 91–92
Gopher, 29
Goûts de France, 63
government agencies, 25, 29, 40,
   94
Greece, 45
Guide, 31

hackers, 71, 75–77
Hallmark.com, 65
harassment, 70, 72–76
Harris, Eric, 70–72
Harvard University, 18, 60
health care, 37, 94
Herzfeld, Charles, 24
high-speed networks, 37, 44–45,
   94
High-Technology Crime
   Investigation Association, 81
history, 9–25
Hitchcock, J.A., 68, 72–74, 81
hoaxes, 58
Home Assurance, 87–88
homes, smart, 85–88
hospitals, 37
hosts, 15, 20–26, 36–39, 47
HOSTS.TXT, 25
HTML (hypertext markup language), 32–34
HTTP (hypertext transfer protocol),
   32–34
hubs, 45–46, 48, 51–52
Human-Nets (mailing list), 20
hypertext, 29–34, 38

IBM, 45, 49
ICQ, 56
identity theft, 78, 80
indexing spiders, 29
INET, 50
information, sharing of, 14–34,
   40–43, 58–61
infrastructure, 41–43, 50–52
instant messaging, 43, 56

Institute and Museum of the History of Science, 62
International Conference on Computers and Communication, 20–21
Internet
 control of, 34, 48, 50–52, 70
 future of, 82–95
 history of, 9–25
 structure of, 39–52
 uses of, 7, 19, 37, 53–67
Internet Crimes Against Children Task Force, 81
Internet Explorer, 36
Internet Network Technology Workshop, 50
Internetting Project, 21
Internet2, 94
intranets, 41, 43
IP addresses, 21–22
IRC (Internet Relay Chat), 56
ISDN (integrated services digital network), 45
ISOC (Internet Society), 50–51
ISPs (Internet service providers), 21, 25, 40, 44, 48, 70, 75
Italy, 45

Kahn, Bob, 21
Kaupp, Morgan, 37
Keyhole, Inc., 64
Klebold, Dylan, 71
Kleinrock, Leonard, 15, 17, 82, 91, 93–95
Kline, Charley, 17
K-12 Educational Networking Workshop, 50
Kunz, Paul, 35

languages, foreign, 60–61
 English as, 54–55
LANs (local area networks), 41, 43, 47
law-enforcement agencies, 70–77, 80–81
leisure activities, 7, 61–62
Levin, Vladimir, 77
libraries, 14, 55, 59
Library of Michigan, 59
Licklider, Joseph C.R., 14

light, 42, 94
Light, Paula, 83–84
Lindner, Paul, 29
links, 28–33, 52
log-in, 20
Louvre, 62

magazines, 7, 59
mail, electronic. See e-mail
mailing lists, 20, 23
Margherita 2000, 86
marketing, 90–92
Massachusetts Institute of Technology (MIT), 14–15
McCahill, Mark P., 29
MCI, 45
meatspace, 57
medicine, 37, 94
Merloni, 86
Microsoft, 36, 56, 88, 90, 92
microwave ovens, 86
military, 12–14, 24–25
missiles, nuclear, 13
Mockapetris, Paul, 25
modems, 40
Mosaic, 36
mouse, 26, 32
MSNBC News, 58
MSN Messenger, 56
museums, 7, 61–62
Mystical Unicorn, A (bookstore), 65
myths, 24

Naperville, Illinois, 81
NAPs (network access points), 45–46
National Aeronautics and Space Administration (NASA), 18, 37, 45, 64, 89
National Gallery of Art, 61–62
National Geographic (magazine), 59
National Institutes of Health, 45
National Novel Writing Month (NaNoWriMo) 2004, 83
National Science Foundation (NSF), 18, 45
Net. *See* Internet
netizens, 14
NetMeetings, 43
Netscape Navigator, 36

Network-Hackers (mailing list), 20
networks, 12, 43–45
  global, 14–15, 28, 33–34, 39,
    55–58
  high-speed, 37, 45, 94
  linking of, 9–11, 20–25, 41,
    47–48, 93
  see also specific networks
news, 7, 55, 58–59
newsgroups, 23–24, 34, 43, 56–58,
  72–73
newspapers, 59
New York City, 80
New York Public Library, 60
Next Generation Secure
  Computing Base, 88
nodes, 15, 17, 30
nomadic access, 93
nonprofit organizations, 25
NSFNET, 45
NSPs (network service providers),
  44
  see also ISPs

online reading rooms, 60
online services, 43–44
  see also World Wide Web
Operation Avalanche, 81
Oxford University (England), 60

packets, data, 15–17, 21, 46–47
pages, Web, 32–33, 37–38
  see also Web sites
Palladium. *See* Next Generation
  Secure Computing Base
parallel computing, 49
passwords, 26, 44, 75, 77
PBS.org, 61
PDAs (personal digital assistants), 93
Peapod.com, 65, 87
personal computers (PCs), 9
phishing, 78
phonographs, 53
photographs, 19, 64, 94
phreaking, 71
Picturephone, 19
point and click, 26, 33
police, 73, 80–81
PrimaryGames.com, 61
printers, sharing of, 41

privacy, 88, 90–91
Prodigy, 43
programmers, 26, 34, 76
programs, 29–32, 47
  see also software
Project Gutenberg, 59
protocols, 15, 21, 34, 47–48, 50, 89,
  93
PuzzleFactory.com, 61

Quigley's Rare Books, 65

radio, 9, 53
Raines, Mary, 54–55, 63
Rasmussen, Jennifer, 8–9
refrigerators, 86–87
research, 24, 59–61
robberies, 76–77
routers, 16, 40, 47–48
Royal Radar Establishment, 21
Russia, 45

San Diego, California, 81
satellite imagery, 64
satellite links, 9, 21, 37, 41, 44, 94
satellites, 13, 44, 49
search engines, 28–29, 59–60
Seattle, Washington, 81
security, 15, 17, 47, 51–52, 71,
  76–78, 88–91
senior citizens, 87–88
servers, 29, 32–33, 35, 41
SF-Lovers (mailing list), 20
Sharp Electronics Corporation, 86
shill bidding, 79
shopping, 7, 62–63, 65, 87
Sioux Falls, South Dakota, 81
sites, Web. See Web sites
smart homes, 85–88
smart spaces, 93
SNDMSG, 18, 20
software, 30–31, 35, 86, 88
solar system, 89
Source, 43
Soviet Union, 13–14
  see also Russia
space missions, 13, 37, 89
spam, 88
Sprint, 45
Sputnik (space satellite), 13

stalking. *See* cyberstalking; harassment
Stanford Research Institute (SRI), 17
Stanford University, 60
structure, 39–52
suffixes, 25
supercomputers, 9, 24, 45, 48, 49
surgery, 37
switching equipment, 16, 40, 44

Tastes of France, 63
Taylor, Robert, 14
TCP/IP (transmission-control/Internet protocol), 21–22
teaching, 54–55
techies, 26
telephone lines, 15–17, 40
telephones, 19, 42, 53, 71
  see also cell phones
television, 9, 19, 42, 53
terabits, 49
teraflops, 49
terrorism, 51–52
text messages, 23
Thaddeus Books, 65
ThinkQuest Internet Challenge, 51
thread, 23
threats, 68–72
Tomlinson, Ray, 18
T1 lines, 45
total internal reflection, 42
travel, 63, 64
Truscott, Tom, 23
Trygstad, Randi, 65, 67

United States, 11, 13, 25, 45, 53, 78, 94
universities, 29, 40, 94
  see also individual universities and schools
University College of London, 21
University of California at Los Angeles (UCLA), 17

University of California at Santa Barbara, 18
University of Michigan, 60
University of Minnesota, 29
University of Utah, 18
URI (universal resource identifier), 33–34
URL (universal resource locator), 33
U.S. Department of Defense, 12–13
U.S. Department of Energy, 45
U.S. Postal Service, 65
Usenet, 23–24, 58
users, numbers of, 9–11, 53
uses, 7, 19, 37, 53–67
UUNET, 45

Veronica (search tool), 29
video streaming, 19
Virtual Collaborative Clinic, 37
virtual reality, 14, 21, 37, 64, 82–85, 95
viruses, 88
voting, 7

Wall Street Journal (newspaper), 59
Walton, Kenneth, 79
WAP (Wireless Application Protocol), 93
washing machines, 86
weather, 49
Web. *See* World Wide Web
Web sites, 32–33, 36–38, 58–65, 68–72, 88, 91–93
Wine-Tasters (mailing list), 20
wireless technology, 41, 87–88, 93–94
wires, 9, 19, 41–42, 94
workstations, 41
WorldCom, 45
World Wide Web, 26–38, 43–44, 53
writing, 83–84

Yahoo!, 57, 61, 92
Youens, Liam, 68–70

Picture Credits

About the Author

Peggy J. Parks holds a bachelor of science degree from Aquinas College in Grand Rapids, Michigan, where she graduated magna cum laude. She is a freelance writer and author who has written more than forty titles for Thomson Gale's Lucent Books, Blackbirch Press, and KidHaven Press imprints. Her books cover a wide range of topics, including global warming, astronomy, the Great Depression, Middle Eastern conflict, scientific achievers, famous world landmarks, natural wonders, and career exploration. Parks lives in Muskegon, Michigan, a town that she says inspires her writing because of its location on the shores of Lake Michigan.